GSA Schedules

The Shortest Path to Federal Dollars

Richard White

Cover design: Thomas Luparello

1

Foreword

This book is written for companies trying to crack the federal market, companies that already sell in the federal market but want to increase sales, and companies that currently hold GSA Schedule contracts but want to understand and manage their contracts better.

Richard White is an authority on federal sales and the author of Rolling the Dice in DC: How the Federal Sales Game is Really Played. Companies selling successfully in the federal market play the federal sales game using multi-vendor, approved price list contracts like GSA Schedules. GSA Schedules are the best way for newcomers to break into this huge market. Read this book and learn how to play the game like the insiders do.

Many of the Internet sites referenced in this book have url's that go on forever and are too long for inclusion in the text. In these cases, we have underlined the title of the Internet site. Use the search engine of your choice to find the site.

Table of Contents

APPENDICES

Chapter 1

Understanding the GSA Schedule

The federal government purchases roughly $500 billion in products and services annually. Insiders who know how to play the federal sales game dominate the market. Why not become an insider and share in this huge pot of gold?

Federal sales through General Services Administration (GSA) Schedule contracts are expected to reach around $40 billion in 2008. GSA Schedules list a company's approved federal prices and provide ordering procedures for use by any federal buyer. Although contract holders still have to sell their products and services, GSA Schedules provide federal buyers with a quick way to close a federal sale while at the same time staying within the federal rules for competition when making buys with public money.

Having a GSA Schedule contract gives companies an edge in making sales, and cuts down the competition—to almost none at times. Compared to buys made through a public bidding process, orders under a Schedule contract are more or less hidden from view. Most importantly, GSA Schedule contracts are open to small businesses. What more could a company trying to crack the federal market want?

In order to become an "insider" in the federal sales game, you must have a thorough understanding of the market. Federal buyers are spending public money and must follow specific rules and regulations to ensure that there is competition between vendors to obtain value for the taxpayer. Note that I said rules to ensure "competition between vendors"—not all possible vendors—and "obtain value"—not the absolute best value. Competition among all possible vendors and obtaining the absolute best value are federal procurement goals, but are not economically feasible in practice. It would take too long to make a purchase, and in the long run is not in the best interest of the taxpayer. Drinking water and trailers would never get to disaster victims if those goals were held to be of primary importance for every purchase.

To become an insider, your company must hold a direct contract with a federal agency. A federal contract gives your business the opportunity to demonstrate, through your partnership with the federal agency, that your product or service provides value to federal buyers. It allows you to become a proven vendor and valued partner.

Vendor partnerships become the path of least resistance for federal buyers. It minimizes the federal buyer's risk and enables buyers to obtain what they want quickly and efficiently. As in the commercial market, federal buyers go with the proven vendor. Think about it. You do the same thing when purchasing goods or services. By becoming a tried-and-true, valued partner, insiders continue to win federal business and continue to grow and grow.

Obtaining a GSA Schedule allows a company to become an insider quickly because it is a direct federal contract, not a subcontract with an entrenched market insider.

The title of this book is ***The Shortest Path to Federal Dollars: GSA Schedules.*** Note the title says the shortest path; this does not mean that GSA Schedules are the only path or that the path is easy to follow. However, for small businesses that are newcomers to the federal marketplace, obtaining a GSA Schedule is the most efficient way to break into the ranks of the insiders.

The Public Purchasing Dilemma

Here's the dilemma faced by the federal government. Let's say terrorists have attacked a major city in the U.S., or a massive hurricane has hit a low-lying coastal city. Emergency supplies and services need to be rushed to the affected area immediately. A federal buyer can't say, "I can get the purchase made in 60 to 180 days if we really put the screws on. Here's what I'll do":

- Write a specification

- Publish the procurement at our federal public bid Internet site

- Give companies a reasonable amount of time to respond

- Evaluate the bid responses and develop a thick file justifying the purchase

- Order from the winning bidder

- Fight the losing bidders in a "red tape war"

Sixty to 180 days—or even longer—is not going to be acceptable to disaster victims with nowhere to sleep, no clean drinking water, and no electricity. Congress and the public will be up in arms, bemoaning the incompetence and unpreparedness of the government, and the media will be having a field day excoriating the feds for ineptness.

Alternatively, in the face of an emergency, it would make sense if the federal buyer could just pick up the phone and make a sole source purchase from a known supplier. But the last time the buyer did that, some publicity hound in Congress raised a hue and cry over sole sourcing with the taxpayer's dollars. This approach to making purchases just doesn't work that well anymore although it is still practiced behind the scenes.

The GSA Solution

What do commercial companies with recurring needs for products and services do? They pre-negotiate prices, sign a contract stipulating the prices, and use the agreed upon price to buy when the need occurs. Commercial companies call these pre-negotiated agreements approved purchasing lists or approved catalogs.

That's precisely what a GSA Schedule contract is: A pre-negotiated price and ordering procedure, under a blanket contract, that any federal agency can use. It works for the government, for the vendors, and for the taxpayers. Yes, the prices may be a bit higher than if the whole process took 60 to 180 days, but it is quick, efficient, and mirrors the real world of commercial sales.

Here's what GSA says about Schedule contracts:

> *Currently, the GSA Schedules Program is enormous. The Program is designed to enable Federal Agencies to purchase commercial products and*

services quickly, efficiently, and at fair and reasonable prices. It enables Federal Agencies to comply with all Federal Acquisition Regulations (FAR) when "easy-to-use" ordering procedures have been followed. The commercial products and services awarded under GSA Schedule contracts are divided into 53 distinct Schedules. In total, there are over 18,700 MAS (Multiple Award Schedule) contracts in place, covering over 11,000,000 items, so competition is fierce. Each year, several thousand firms submit offers, and over 3,000 are awarded MAS contracts.

Under the GSA Schedules Program, GSA establishes long-term government wide contracts with commercial firms to provide access to over 10 million commercial supplies and services that can be ordered directly from GSA Schedule contractors or through the GSA Advantage!® online shopping and ordering system.

The Program helps reduce acquisition lead time and provides a wide selection of the state-of-the-art commercial supplies and services. GSA has already determined prices to be fair and reasonable and purchases conducted under the GSA Schedule Program do not require a synopsis (public announcement) of the requirement. Although GSA provides information material on the benefits of the Program, GSA does not market or promote specific contracts, does not distribute products of individual firms, and does not steer business to any individual contractor.

Sounds simple, doesn't it? Read on.

Chapter 2

GSA Schedules: The Super Stars of Multi-Vendor Contracts

A multi-vendor contract is a pre-negotiated contract awarded to a number of vendors before specific purchasing requirements are known. Vendor's prices are negotiated up-front and listed in the contract. Thus, the federal rules presume that the competition took place during contract negotiations. When the need for a product or service arises, the contracting officer or end-user can turn to the list of pre-approved vendors, solicit a limited number of bids, and make a purchase quickly and efficiently.

In this way, the time and expense involved with a public bid are avoided because the vendors holding this type of contract have agreed-upon price lists that become the basis for bids on individual task orders (services) or delivery orders (products). Buyers can avoid a costly and incredibly time-consuming public bid, while still adhering to the ideal of full and open competition—at least on paper.

The federal government would grind to a halt without multi-vendor contracts. They limit competition but speed up the buying process and make it cheaper for the taxpayer. Limiting competition is not a bad thing, because the reality is that most big-buck public bids have already been pre-sold by one or more vendors prior to the bid being issued; the real competition takes place among the pre-sellers. Inexperienced vendors waste a lot of money writing proposals that never had a prayer in the first place when they respond blindly to public bids.

GSA Schedules are the most widely used and well known of the multi-vendor contracts.

The Ins and Outs of GSA Schedules

The General Services Administration (GSA) initiated the Schedules program, also known as the Federal Supply Schedule program, to simplify the process of acquiring needed goods and services.

A Schedule contract is a five-year contract containing three, five-year renewal options. In total, if the government were to exercise all three options, the term of the contract would span 20 years. Although a Schedule contract is an official federal contract, no money passes hands until a purchase order is actually placed through the contract. As such, the onus is on the Schedule contract holder to actively solicit orders from federal buyers.

A Schedule contractor must meet GSA's $25,000 minimum threshold in annual sales or run the risk of having the contract terminated. GSA funds the Schedules program by assessing an "Industrial Funding Fee" of 0.75% on each dollar sold under a vendor's GSA Schedule contract. Vendors must report their Schedule sales to GSA on a quarterly basis and pay the appropriate Industrial Funding Fee at that time.

At present, there are 53 categories of products and services sold to the government under the Schedules program. This includes office products, information technology equipment, building supplies, medical equipment, chemical supplies, and a host of professional services such as management consulting, accounting, and professional engineering services. The Schedule program does not cover certain industries, such as architectural design or construction services.

The Federal Acquisition Service (FAS) administers the GSA Schedule program. Nine centers spread throughout the United States manage the program. (See Appendix A for the specific duties and contact information for each of the GSA Schedule Management Centers.) GSA centers perform the following management functions:

- Process and evaluate proposals that vendors have submitted for GSA Schedule consideration

- Award contracts

- Administer contracts; including signing contract modifications for price changes, product and service additions and deletions, monitoring IFF payments, etc.

Applying for a Schedule Contract

In order to get on the inside government sales track with a Schedule contract, a vendor must go through an arduous application process. The most difficult and painstaking part of the Schedule application and approval process is negotiating what the government and vendor agree is a "fair and reasonable price" for the vendor's products or services. Because of the complexity of the undertaking, vendors sometimes choose to hire consultants to assist in the preparation and negotiation of the contract. Many report that the expense of hiring a consultant was money well spent, because the entire submission and approval process can be extremely costly in terms of time and energy, and very daunting for the uninitiated.

Once a Schedule contract is awarded, the successful vendor is placed on a list of approved suppliers for that particular Schedule. Federal agency buyers can then order from a vendor using GSA Advantage!, the government's online "shopping mall" for GSA Schedule products and services. A common misconception is that only GSA employees can make a purchase through a Schedule contract. This is not true; virtually any federal buyer can buy from GSA Schedule holders. Congress has also granted state and local agencies the authority to make purchases through the Information Technology Schedule contract (known as the "IT 70 Schedule"). State and local purchasing authority may be extended to other GSA Schedules in the future. Recently, Congress authorized the use of all Schedules by state and local government under emergency conditions and state and local purchases may be made from Schedule 84 Total Solutions for Law Enforcement at any time.

Ease of Use

Making a purchase through a Schedule contract is relatively easy. A federal buyer interested in a particular product or service sends a Request for Quote to companies holding a GSA Schedule contract for the desired product or service. In response, each company's GSA point person prepares a quote using its approved GSA Schedule contract prices. The buyer makes a final decision as to which vendor to use, and then places a purchase order against the vendor's GSA Schedule contract. The purchase order is then sent directly to the vendor.

There is significantly less competition in the GSA Schedule arena than there is for a bid put out as a public procurement because buyers only need to procure three quotes from GSA Schedule holders prior to making a purchase, and the three prospective vendors' pricing was determined during negotiations prior to contract award.

This illusion of reduced competition can be deceptive though. Many vendors new to the system assume that once awarded a contract, purchase orders will begin to roll in without the necessity of any further action on their part. This expectation is unrealistic. Schedule contract holders must actively sell their company's capabilities to prospective federal buyers. Schedule vendors should not expect to make sales under their Schedule contracts without focused and tenacious agency-based sales efforts.

Schedule Pros and Cons

Because purchasing from a Schedule vendor is quick and efficient, sales under the Schedules program are skyrocketing. GSA's Information Technology Division, the most successful division in the program, reports that fiscal year 2006 sales for their division alone totaled approximately $17 billion. Federal buyers report that pre-negotiated pricing is one of the key factors to the success of the program. Furthermore, buyers rave about the efficiency of the process and the significant reduction in paperwork and red tape associated with Schedule buys. Lastly, Schedule purchases are essentially transacted behind the scenes without much scrutiny from non-participating vendors. This lack of transparency cuts down on costly vendor protests.

Vendors like Schedule contracts for the same reasons that federal buyers do. The Schedule program reduces competition, allows vendors to avoid public bids (saving vast amounts of money in proposal development costs), and allows contractors to close a deal within weeks instead of waiting months on end for an award of a public bid.

Equally important, federal buyers like them, and sales people like what buyers like.

GSA Schedule contracts do have drawbacks. Obtaining one can cost in excess of $15,000, and could necessitate hiring proposal writers, or moving billable workers to unbillable work. The return on this investment is low unless a company has substantial annual Schedule contract sales. Other drawbacks include:

- Your ability to increase your GSA contract prices is restricted by the terms of the contract.

- The terms of the Schedule contract require that vendors carefully monitor and control their commercial discounting practices. Indiscriminate or random, one-time commercial discounting can lead to automatic reductions in GSA contract prices. The primary reason most companies decide not to pursue a GSA Schedule is the loss (to varying degrees) of discounting flexibility. The loss of flexibility can be minimized through effective negotiations with GSA, but not eliminated entirely. This can be a problem for those companies that "price to close." Loss of discounting flexibility can affect sales negatively, especially in industries where market discounts are a way of life.

- If a business does not meet the annual sales threshold of $25,000, its GSA Schedule contract can be terminated.

- Schedule orders must be carefully tracked and accounted for to ensure that the proper Industrial Funding Fee is paid at the end of each quarter.

GSA sales costs can be high for companies new to the federal market. During price negotiations, GSA will argue that it is the world's biggest customer. However, winning a Schedule contract really just gives a company the right to try to sell to federal agencies. Pursuing sales with multiple agencies can be expensive for a company starting from scratch.

Drawbacks aside, a GSA Schedule is the selling vehicle of choice if a company intends to sell through a single, multiple award contract. An aggressive company willing to devote dollar and staff resources to developing federal business can reap great rewards through its GSA Schedule contract.

Chapter 3

Pursuing a GSA Schedule: It's All in the Details

GSA Schedule solicitations are unique in that they are always open and a vendor may submit a proposal at any time. Normally, federal solicitations for products and services have a closing date for proposal submittal. The opportunity to submit a bid at any time is what makes the GSA Schedule program attractive to small businesses. However, the "always open" aspect of GSA Schedule solicitations does have one downside. Companies considering submitting a proposal to GSA can procrastinate, procrastinate, and procrastinate some more, often taking a year or more to prepare and submit a proposal.

A business of any size, provided it is stable, financially sound, and has a sales history, can get on the GSA Schedule. This is not true for other types of multi-vendor contracts. Most other multi-vendor contracts are open for bid for a specific period of time and then the game is over. Either you beat the other vendors competing for the contract or you didn't. In effect, you are competing against yourself when you submit a proposal for a GSA Schedule contract. Your corporate experience and willingness to negotiate prices that the government will accept determines whether you receive a contract. With some exceptions, the other multi-vendor contracts are either held by the big guys or by socially or economically disadvantaged businesses.

How GSA Orders Are Placed

GSA Schedules are also unique in that purchases are transacted directly between the federal agency requiring a product or service and the contractor. Any federal agency, anywhere in the world, can place an order using the prices, ordering procedures, and terms and conditions specified in the Schedule contract. Once a need is identified, the contracting officer of the ordering agency simply places the order.

You and your sales force need to keep in mind that GSA contracting officers and the contracting officer within an agency placing an order have very different roles. GSA contracting officers evaluate your proposal, negotiate pricing, award, and administer contracts; they are not involved in the ordering process. Their job is to set up contracts with the best price possible and a nice thick file demonstrating that all federal procurement rules have been followed. After contract award, GSA contracting officers focus on administering Schedule contracts.

Although the contracting officer with the ordering agency is following the same rule book as the GSA contracting officer, the two have fundamentally different roles and it is important for your sales force to understand the difference. The GSA contracting officer wants to ensure that procurement policy has been followed to the letter and, somewhat secondarily, that purchasing goes smoothly. The contracting officer for the ordering agency wants to place an order quickly and receive products and services as soon as possible. That's why the order was placed using a GSA Schedule in the first place. If an open item—one not on your Schedule—sneaks into the order, so be it.

Fitting Schedules to Companies

"Which GSA Schedule fits my company?" That's usually the first question vendors ask, and it's the million-dollar question. The products and services covered by each of the 53 or so Schedules are listed at www.gsa.gov. Follow the "GSA Schedules" links and review the product/service categories to determine which Schedule would be appropriate for your company. Sometimes it is clear and sometimes it isn't. It will be clear for office supplies or office furniture, but not so clear for training and professional services.

In some cases the lists of products and services covered under the 53 GSA Schedules are ambiguous. Although GSA didn't set out to purposely frustrate companies, the resulting scopes of work for the 53 Schedules are confusing. For example:

Some products and services that might logically be categorized under a particular Schedule fall under a seemingly unrelated Schedule. For instance, if a company wanted to sell rifle scopes to improve a shooter's accuracy, it might need to get on a law enforcement Schedule to sell weapon accessories, and an IT Schedule to sell the software that runs the scope. In other words, assignment of products and services to particular Schedules can be artificial and arbitrary.

GSA couldn't list every type of product and service, so some products and services have to be "read into" the listings. The MOBIS Schedule—Mission Oriented Business Integration Services—is essentially a management consulting contract but a wide range of services are provided under its umbrella.

A particular product or service may be covered by more than one Schedule.

Some companies need more than one Schedule to cover their offerings. A company providing software for loan services and mortgage tracking, might need to have two separate Schedules. A large federal contractor may have many schedules, ranging from training, advertising, and human resources to professional engineering services.

Schedule contracts are not available for architectural and engineering services, for construction (unless it is related to installing a product), or for research and development.

GSA created a Consolidated Schedule (00CORP) for companies needing more than one Schedule to cover their offerings. It's a step toward a single GSA Schedule for all products and services, but it falls short in its coverage.

To make matters worse, several years ago procurement policy violations related to GSA Schedules came to light during the Abu Ghraib prison scandal in Iraq. An Army investigation identified employees of a federal contractor as interrogators implicated in the torture and abuse of prisoners. The interrogators were hired under an information technology GSA schedule.

The scandal caused GSA to become extremely sensitive to the "fit" of a company's products and services to a particular Schedule. This has increased the rate of proposal rejections based on scope of work issues (the "fit" of a product or service to a particular Schedule). Small businesses spend considerable amounts of money developing GSA Schedule proposals and a proposal rejection can be a major financial blow.

Answering the question "Which GSA Schedule fits my company?" requires experience and tenacity. The quagmire of GSA Schedule scope of work and red tape issues has spawned an entire industry of GSA Schedule consultants, present company included. Selecting the right Schedule for your company is crucial. If GSA rejects your proposal and you have to start over … let's just say that rewriting a 150-page proposal is not fun.

Once you have identified the right Schedule, read and make sure you understand the solicitation. The terms and conditions the solicitation contains are the rules for contract performance and administration that you will have to follow if you receive a GSA Schedule contract.

Schedule-Speak: A New Foreign Language

Small businesses new to federal contracting almost always find the language in GSA Schedules mysterious, confusing, and impenetrable. Many prospective contractors complain of difficulties navigating the GSA website and finding the list of products and services covered by GSA Schedules. Others complain about the challenge of identifying the Solicitation or Request for Proposal (RFP) that applies to their company's products or services. The persistent few able to trudge through these difficulties and find the appropriate solicitation often discover that it seems to be written in a foreign language.

GSA Schedule solicitations are definitely not reader-friendly. They contain strange, unfamiliar terms and are written in what we call (not too fondly) "government-speak." Most solicitations exceed 150 pages in length, and are printed in blindingly small font. Some of the more important sections and their shortcomings include:

- Standard boilerplate federal contract clauses often create an ominous impression when in fact the clauses are reasonably innocuous.

- Some clauses are far more important than others, yet they're all given equal weight. The critical clauses are discussed in-depth in this book.

- The language in the Certifications and Representations section is difficult to interpret. In spite of the difficulty, the prospective contractor (also known as the "Offeror") is legally required to certify that statements made in the proposal are accurate and true.

- Proposal preparation instructions are often far too short and even more often confusing.

- The section pertaining to how proposals will be evaluated is too brief.

- The provisions pertaining to the post-award process and the expectations of the contractor once an award is granted are unclear. Little or no time is spent educating new contractors on their responsibilities to the government.

What Drives Companies to Pursue GSA Schedules

Sales numbers for a particular Schedule may be interesting to look at, but the numbers are all large and not particularly useful to individual companies. (That being said, if you're still interested, Appendix B provides vendor sales by GSA Schedule.) The size of a particular GSA Schedule market is not a meaningful number if only a tiny slice of the market is actually available to your company. A laundry services company in the Chicago area has a limited geographic area in which it can realistically deliver its services. The key question for this type of company is "Are there federal offices or installations in our locale, and do these entities need our services?"

Once that question is addressed, the next question becomes "How much of the available work is currently held by incumbent contractors, and how much of it is new work?" By doing research, your company should be able to make a reasonable estimate of the available contract dollars within reach of your company.

A company selling office supplies rather than services has a different set of questions to answer because office supplies can be sold by telephone to virtually any federal customer regardless of location. The critical questions are:

- Where should we focus our efforts when attempting to sell to a federal customer?

- When and how does price enter into the picture?

- What importance does the customer place on service?

- How difficult is it to replace an entrenched office supply company and how can it be done?

The deciding factor in whether or not to go after a Schedule contract is the determination of how much you can actually sell under a Schedule.

However, it's not just size of market that drives a company to pursue a GSA Schedule. Companies attending our GSA Schedule proposal preparation workshop tell us that they decided to pursue a Schedule contract for the following reasons:

- The company currently does business with the federal government, and their contracting officer told them to get a Schedule to make it easier to transact purchases. In some cases, contracting officers go as far as to say you have to get a Schedule contract if you want to continue doing business with us.

- The company worked as a subcontractor to a federal prime contractor. The agency is now getting tired of paying prime contractor mark-ups and has recommended that the subcontracting company obtain their own Schedule contract. Alternatively, the company tired of the yoke of a prime contractor and wants to work with the customer directly to increase the probability—and profitability—of new business.

- The company has studied the federal market and decided that a Schedule is the best way to close deals.

Fedmarket.com sells GSA Schedule services and has a built-in bias for Schedules. But obtaining a GSA Schedule contract for your company involves money, intense staff involvement in writing the proposal, and a lot of red tape. Obviously, you would make the investment only if you thought the GSA Schedule would increase your revenue. The question is much bigger than "Should we get a Schedule contract?" The critical question is "Are we serious about the federal market and are we willing to do what it takes to win federal business?"

We ask the following questions when companies ask us if we think they need a Schedule:

- Are you currently doing business with the feds? Has your contracting officer asked whether you have a GSA Schedule, or suggested that it would be a lot easier to do business if you had one?

- Do your competitors have a Schedule? How much business are they doing under their Schedule?

- Are you doing business with a federal agency under the thumb of a prime contractor and need a way to contract directly with the federal agency?

- Are you new to the federal market and need a way to close a federal sale quickly with minimal competition?

The insiders have Schedules and other multi-vendor contracts. But having a GSA Schedule alone will do nothing to increase your revenue. A GSA Schedule returns the investment many times over if, and only if, you are willing to establish an aggressive federal marketing campaign.

Chapter 4

GSA Schedule Rules: Full and Open Competition

Public bids under the federal government's "full and open competition rules" are horrendously inefficient. End-users and official buyers do not like to use public bids. Once a program administrator has identified a need, or reached a decision to buy a particular product or service, he or she typically wants the product or solution of choice as soon as possible. Bureaucrats are human, and they're not patient.

Public bids require significant amounts of time to prepare the bid documents, write the solicitation, evaluate proposals once they've been submitted, and work through final negotiations to contract award. This process can easily take anywhere from six months to a year. All of this work, combined with the possibility that a losing bidder could protest the contract award, causing even more work and time to elapse, adds up to a general distaste for the public bidding process. It is no surprise, then, that the use of GSA Schedules has skyrocketed in recent years.

GSA designed Schedule procurement rules for speed and efficiency. A highly efficient purchasing procedure may inherently result in less competition and higher prices, but many believe that the net gain in saved time and administrative cost is worth it.

The rules governing GSA Schedules are set out in Federal Acquisition Regulation (FAR) Subpart 8.4. They can be accessed at http://www.arnet.gov/far/. Hopefully, this section of the book will keep you from having to read Subpart 8.4. The key points of the GSA Schedule regulations from a sales perspective are:

- GSA determines the price of items under Schedule contracts prior to contract award and considers these prices to be fair and reasonable.

- Orders placed by individual federal agencies are therefore considered to be purchases made in an arena of full and open competition. Federal buyers do not need to seek further competition or consider small business programs. For service task orders and some product orders, contracting officers must seek several quotes from GSA Schedule vendors. Real competition may or may not be achieved when multiple quotes are sought. At the very least, a "paper competition" has taken place.

- Federal buyers place orders by using GSA Advantage! or by reviewing the price lists of at least three Schedule contractors.

- Federal buyers are encouraged to seek further price reductions when an order exceeds the maximum order threshold stated in the GSA Schedule contract.

- Vendors are not required to extend price reductions made under a specific GSA Schedule order to other federal agencies ordering under the vendor's contract.

In a nutshell, the regulations say the competition took place when the vendor negotiated its Schedule prices. Price and competition are important in federal purchasing but so are purchasing speed, efficiency, and product/service value. Federal purchasing organizations are notoriously understaffed, and contracting officers seek vendors who make buying easy—and they know purchases can be made quickly and with a minimum of effort from vendors with multi-vendor contracts. Your goal should be to be a company that buyers consider easy to do business with.

Chapter 5

Selling to the Feds

Federal end-users, such as human resource program managers, engineers, or facility managers, make most purchasing decisions. As the term implies, the end-user is the person who will actually use the service. Services and complex products and solutions must be sold to the end-user because that's who will determine whether the service or product meets their needs and solves their problem.

Selling to the federal government mirrors the sales process in the commercial sector. You have to identify the end-users, knock on their door, be prepared for rejection if you are making cold calls, and be persistent. Use existing federal relationships to spawn new relationships if you can.

The difference between selling in the federal market as opposed to the commercial sector is that with the feds it is critical that you have a way to close the sale once the buyer has decided that your product or service is the one that will meet their needs. Closing in this context means signing a contract under federal purchasing rules. That is precisely what a GSA Schedule allows you to do.

Competing for Federal Sales

The amount of competition introduced by purchasing rules can vary from none to a considerable amount, depending on the situation. Federal purchasing rules require more competition—and documentation showing competition—as the size of procurements increase. Rules governing micro-purchases—those under $3,000—allow sole source buys made directly by end-users using a government credit card. The $3,000 limit can be increased to $15,000 or even higher under emergency or special circumstances. Credit card purchases do not have to go through the official contracting office, so that market segment is identical to the commercial market.

Federal contracting officers must transact all other federal purchases. Purchases up to $25,000 can be made with simplified purchasing procedures; the contracting officer only needs to solicit three price quotes, which can be submitted verbally, by fax, or by email. Purchases over $25,000 require full and open competition either through a public bid or use of a multi-vendor contract.

So which comes first, the decision to buy from a specific company or the competition to select a particular vendor? People who know the answer to this question know how to make federal sales.

The answer is not simple. Understanding the reality of federal sales is essential to understanding why GSA Schedules are so critical in the selling process. Under federal rules, companies are free to meet with and sell to federal end-users at any time if purchases are made using a Schedule contract. In cases when a purchase is going to be put out as a public bid, vendors can only meet with federal end-users prior to the bid being issued. There is almost always a back-story behind most federal contract transactions. One or more vendors have probably met with the end-user and these vendors will have an edge over vendors who have not done advance sales. In many cases, it may be far more than an edge.

In the case of complex Information Technology (IT) solutions and services, for instance, the real competition usually takes place before the application of the rules. Say a federal program manager has been working with an IT company called JLW and needs to expand the agency's computing capabilities. Sales people from JLW have met multiple times with the manager, helping to define the problem and suggest solutions. The manager is comfortable with the JLW reps, familiar with the company's products, and wants to work with the company. Even in the face of the competition of a public bid, JLW has a decided advantage.

Keep in mind the roles of the various players. The salesperson's goal is to gain a sales advantage over competitors. The end-user's goal is to make a purchase quickly and efficiently while at the same time minimizing risk by making the buy from a known entity. The contracting officer's goal is to compile a file demonstrating that full and open competition took place— even if it's on paper only.

Assume your competitors are making sales calls to the same end-users you are, and that that's where the real competition takes place.

GSA Contracts: Good in a Pinch

The utility of holding a GSA Schedule is best demonstrated with an example.

Let's say you own an office supplies business located near a military base. You've been calling on the supply manager of the printing center for some time with no success. You know the base has been buying from the same large office supplies company for years.

In late August, it appears that the printing center will have around $300,000 remaining in their annual budget. Adhering to the "use it or lose it" principle, the center doesn't want the $300,000 to go unspent. Furthermore, management needs to meet their annual small business participation goals and the contracting office has been told to get some of their year-end money to small businesses.

The printing center manager calls and asks if you can deliver 10,000 cases of multi-purpose printer paper to the base for around $300,000. He knows paper prices and $30 a case would be a good price for a high volume order. He also mentions that he has several thousand cases in inventory but the base can always use printer paper, it doesn't spoil, and the $300,000 needs to be spent by September 30. "Take your time delivering it since the storeroom is pretty full at this point," he says. "And, oh, by the way, I hope you have a GSA Schedule because we do not have time for a public procurement and this buy needs to be inked ASAP."

You do have a GSA Schedule contract for office supplies, and your pre-negotiated price is $32 per case. But this transaction will make your year and get your foot in the door. So you say, "I can do $30 for 10,000 cases, no problem. My distributor will load up a truck whenever you tell me to deliver." (GSA contracts have an almost built-in expectation that vendors will reduce their pre-negotiated prices for high volume orders.)

Or you don't have a GSA Schedule contract. The printing center manager moves on to another vendor and you're out a windfall sale.

This may seem like an extreme example. But it does illustrate how GSA Schedules work. Lots of year-end money is spent through Schedules every year, and if you don't have one, that sale goes to someone else.

Disaster Buying Scenario

Suppose you are a contracting officer in the Federal Emergency Management Agency (FEMA). Hurricane Katrina leveled New Orleans a week ago. All the people on rooftops have been rescued, but the shelters are full, and the true scope of the disaster is becoming ever more clear. Thousands of trailers need to be delivered ASAP. Media coverage is relentless and the pressure to buy, and buy fast, is tremendous.

As the FEMA contracting officer, you can't use simplified acquisition procedures because the procurement is too large. What are your options? You would love to do a sole source buy, which probably makes sense, but you know someone in Congress and half the howling media will be second-guessing you if there turns out to be a problem with the products you've purchased.

So you research trailer vendors. One trailer vendor with a low price does not have a GSA Schedule or similar multi-vendor contract, so you would probably have to use traditional full and open (read time-consuming, red-tape laden) acquisition procedures. Or you could figure out another way to make the buy—probably through a subcontract with a vendor already holding a contract with the agency. Procedurally neither alternative is particularly attractive; they both take a tremendous amount of paperwork, staff time, and elapsed time. Meanwhile, people are homeless and the entire area has been declared a national disaster.

Another trailer vendor has a GSA Schedule contract and a higher price. This vendor could meet the end-user's needs in a matter of a week or so and you could do the purchase quickly. As the contracting officer in this scenario, which vendor are you going to choose?

Competition among GSA Schedule Holders

Most companies worry about their competitors; as Andy Grove says, "Only the paranoid survive." Here is GSA's take on dealing with the competition on GSA Schedule contracts:

Identify your competitors. Visit the Schedules e-Library website at www.gsaelibrary.gsa.gov and the GSA Advantage website at www.gsaadvantage.gov. These websites contain information regarding the products and services that current [Multiple Award Schedule] MAS contractors already offer. This will aid you in identifying potential competitors under the MAS Program and help you to further assess your ability to compete for orders, if your company is awarded a MAS contract. You should look at such key information as your competitors' pricing, delivery time, warranty terms, services, and other conditions. Think about how you will be prepared to meet or beat such terms. In addition, you should examine other factors that purchasers under the MAS Program may consider when awarding an order such as your company's past performance and expertise in providing the products and/or services that your company is seeking to offer. Often, purchasers under the MAS Program make their award decision based upon "best value" as opposed to lowest price technically acceptable, so you need to assess your ability to compete for orders under all possible award evaluation criteria.

Then, visit our Schedule Sales Query website at http://ssq.gsa.gov/ that provides detailed sales information on current MAS contractors. Specifically, you can search to see whether your competitors have successfully sold similar products and/or services under the MAS Program.

Your review and analysis of these websites should allow you to assess the competitive environment for the products and/or services you want to provide. Once you understand the terms you will have to follow and the market you will operate in, you can decide whether a MAS contract is the right investment for your company to make.

In reality, competition among Schedule holders looks a little different. Is there competition among GSA Schedule holders? Like everything else in federal sales, the answer is yes, no, and maybe, depending on who you talk to.

The GSA language implies that competition takes place when a Request for Quote (RFQ) is issued. As discussed earlier, in most cases, the actual competition takes place way before then. Except for commodities, the competition takes place when a salesperson calls on an end-user and sells a company's products or services based on features and benefits, best value considerations, and by assuring the contracting officer that hiring your company is a minimal risk.

GSA also says competition takes place when they select a vendor from the GSA Advantage electronic mall. Here's how it works.

Say you run a warehouse and need some bookends. You go online to the electronic mall and find that bookend prices range from $1.59 to $52. The cheapest bookends are too flimsy to serve your purpose; the $52 solid wood cherry bookends are a tad excessive for the application. All of the vendors can deliver within four days. In theory, you would randomly pick the vendor with bookends that most closely fit your use and price range.

The reality is that the vendor who has been supplying you for years has bookends that fall within your price range, although they're a little more expensive than the closest competitors'. But you know the quality of the merchandise you're going to get from your trusted vendor, and you know that if there are any problems with the delivery or the product, that your favored vendor will take care of it for you. In this scenario, the real competition took place when the product vendor established a personal relationship with the end-user and sold him or her on the features and benefits of their product and presents their best value proposition.

Orders can come in when a buyer goes to the *GSA Advantage!* e-mall and orders a truckload of toner cartridges based solely on getting the lowest possible unit price. Miracles do happen. But the real competition comes in establishing the customer relationship in the first place. The battle is for the end-user—getting the meeting and elbowing other vendors to the side early in the sales process.

Many vendors new to the federal marketplace believe that a low price will win, and hope to make sales by blindly responding to a Request for Quote (RFQ).

Hope is the operative word here. It can happen if you're selling a commodity like toner cartridges, or in special cases, such as purchases made quickly in response to a natural disaster. But if you haven't already met with the customer/end-user, don't bother responding to an RFQ asking for an "Analysis of the Socio-Economic Issues Resulting from Terrorism in a Third World Country." You have no shot.

Assessing the Competition

More than one company with a GSA Schedule contract may be engaging the end-user, but not all the competitors on your GSA Schedule will be a factor in most cases. An end-user may issue an RFQ to companies he or she is already working with and to companies randomly picked off the list at the electronic mall. The companies already working with the end-user are the ones you should worry about. Companies that receive an RFQ from an unknown end-user are often serving as cannon fodder, providing the paperwork for the contracting officer's file proving that competition took place. To be successful in the federal marketplace:

- You need to generate the demand for your products and services with end-users. The hundreds or even thousands of companies on your Schedule are just names in the database. You only need to worry about the ones that are actively selling against you.

- Only companies with proactive salespeople survive in the federal sales game.

- Think of a GSA Schedule as a tool to close sales, not an opportunity to send in blind bids in response to RFQs. You need to determine whether your company can afford the lead time and expense of implementing an effective federal sales program before pursuing a Schedule contract.

These basic issues in no way imply that you shouldn't concern yourself with who is on your Schedule and their prices. Pricing plays a more significant role in creating competition in commodity purchases versus services buys. Government buyers can readily compare prices for commodities at the *GSA Advantage!* mall; and they actually do (sometimes).

How do you play the price game if you are a commodity player? By offering best value. A good salesperson can make the sale of a case of printer paper into a best value situation by selling service, quality, responsiveness, and liberal return policies.

The Pre-Selling Imperative

GSA schedules are available for a wide range of professional services. In the commercial marketplace, labor rates correlate directly with staff experience and the resumes of specific staff members proposed for a project. In addition to education and experience, the hourly rate charged for a particular consultant or employee is based on the qualifications and the past performance of the consultant's company.

As a result, the government recognized that it is difficult and ultimately unproductive for a federal end-user to try to determine whether a senior management consultant with specific experience related to the project at hand is worth $80 or $85 per hour. Therefore, the federal government decided to accept reality and allow service vendors to get their service rates pre-approved.

Approved Schedule service rates are based on the labor rates a company charges its commercial customers. In essence, the federal government has decided that it will allow the commercial marketplace to drive the service rates. Pre-approved rates for service categories simplify and speed up the procurement process, which ultimately results in savings to the taxpayers.

Federal buyers are required to meet with all vendors interested in selling their services to the government. These meetings take place, but usually when the vendor knocks on the end-user's door; not vice versa.

From a sales point of view, meeting with the end-user is essential to winning business. Solutions and purchases are based on user requirements and these requirements cannot be understood merely by reading the official solicitation. Building face-to-face relationships is imperative.

From the agency buyer's point of view, pre-selling familiarizes the end-user with the services a vendor has to offer and get a handle on the company's experience and the experience of key staff members.

The critical question from a sales viewpoint is: Does pre-selling services to federal end-users give the most aggressive and experienced vendors an advantage? The answer is a resounding "Yes." Is this unfair? Every vendor has an equal opportunity to make a sales call. Pre-selling is simply the reality of what has to be done to sell complex products and service-based solutions.

The Fixed Price Dilemma

Today, most GSA service task orders are fixed price, and the government is putting more and more emphasis on obtaining fixed price contracts every day. When task orders are fixed price, hourly rates do not play a major role in who gets the business.

Contractors are usually not overly concerned about low hourly rates when selling fixed price work because they can influence the price by the number of hours used to justify the price (10,000 hours at $100/hour equals $1,000,000—as does 12,500 hours at $80/hour. Remember that service work is usually sold, not ordered, and the seller usually has an opportunity to influence the specifications for the work.

The rush by the federal government to encourage fixed price service contracts makes sense in theory. But real life is not theoretical. Contractors that sell services are typically involved in establishing specifications and prices. The federal government has great difficulty in writing fixed price specifications on their own, and until they can (probably never), the rush to fixed price contracts is in the contractor's favor, not the government's.

The use of fixed price contracting should be restricted to situations where the government actually writes a tight, realistic specification. However, it will probably be a long time before we see realistic federal specifications.

Chapter 6

The Push-Pull for Small Business Preferences

Throughout this book, we stress that GSA Schedules are ideal mechanisms for small businesses to close their federal sales once an end-user has been sold on the value of their products and services. That doesn't mean that GSA and federal agencies making purchases using GSA Schedules actually favor small businesses.

When evaluating proposals, GSA doesn't take the size of a business into account. They are unbiased in this sense. However, GSA is not particularly excited about receiving offers from small businesses. Small businesses do not generate a lot of Industrial Funding Fees (IFF) and often struggle to compete with entrenched federal contractors. GSA's funding comes from the IFF money, and businesses that do not generate a lot of fees are not GSA favorites, regardless of size.

So on the one hand, GSA doesn't purposely discriminate against small businesses and, in fact, has set aside pieces of Schedules for small businesses only. On the other hand, GSA is trying to reduce the number of companies with low Schedule sales and this indirectly discriminates against small businesses. GSA might dispute this point since it is politically incorrect not to be for small businesses. Take a look at the number of contracts awarded to small businesses listed in Appendix B and judge for yourself.

Solicitation requirements can vary from one RFP to the next. See Appendix C to get an idea of the range. Two common requirements across most Schedules are:

- A company has been in business for at least two years; in some Schedules, the requirement is three years.

- A company submitting a proposal for a services Schedule must have completed projects demonstrating their qualifications within the past two years.

GSA has been tightening its years-in-business and financial requirements recently. This cuts down on the number of small businesses that can submit an offer. However, again, it's not so much a question of discriminating against small businesses as GSA's desire to maximize the Industrial Funding Fees that come with big Schedule sales.

Contract Cancellation for Lack of Sales

The following clause is contained in every GSA Schedule contract in one form or another:

> *A contract will not be awarded unless anticipated sales are expected to exceed at least $25,000 within the first 24 months following contract award, and are expected to exceed $25,000 in sales each 12-month period thereafter. The government may cancel the contract if these sales goals are not met.*

Small businesses, particularly those not certified under a preference program, often have difficulty gaining traction in the federal market. GSA cancels many contracts with small businesses under the minimum $25,000 in annual sales clause. Again, judge for yourself whether this clause is small business friendly. More importantly, determine whether hitting the $25,000 annual sales mark is one that you will struggle to reach before deciding whether to pursue a Schedule contract.

Congressional Intent and Follow-Through

Congress and the regulations associated with specific pieces of legislation require that purchasing agencies set small businesses goals. Theoretically, all buys below $100,000 are set aside for small business. The $100,000 rule does not apply to GSA Schedule purchases. Congress has also authorized a number of small business preference programs that allow sole source buys under certain circumstances; for example, purchases made from small disadvantaged businesses, or disabled veteran-owned businesses. These are laudable programs and they work.

How do the government's small business goals affect your company? Unfortunately, there is no real oversight or authority to enforce these goals. In addition, the rule that procurements under $100,000 have to be set aside for small businesses does not apply to GSA Schedule purchases. A $20,000 purchase can be transacted with a large business even if a small business can provide the same product or service. Again, GSA is not purposely discriminating against small business. The rule is designed to allow speed and efficiency of purchasing.

The problem is that at a gut level, individual end-users prefer large businesses, because they feel like they know them, can trust them, and deep down believe using a known entity minimizes any risk that something might go wrong with a contract. The small business goals, set-asides, and preference programs exist to facilitate the inclusion of small business in the federal marketplace, but implementation is frequently more of an afterthought than the result of actual intent.

Chapter 7

Playing Well with Others:
Teaming Advantages

The GSA Schedule program accommodates almost any type of commercial sales practice, including teaming, reselling, and multi-layered distribution systems. The Schedule program encourages both buyers and sellers to use Schedules creatively and in ways that mirror sales made in the commercial market.

Participating Dealer Agreements

GSA Schedules can accommodate products sold by resellers. Your business might elect to use resellers for a number of reasons: your product is a component of a larger system or larger product, your commercial sales are made through resellers, or your company's budget doesn't allow for a direct sales force.

Participating Dealer Agreements (PDAs) are an effective mechanism to allow other parties to resell your products while you maintain control of your GSA pricing. A PDA is a written agreement between your company and the reseller that formalizes the business deal between the two parties. A PDA generally provides that the reseller will sell your product at the government-approved prices in your GSA Schedule. The PDA establishes the sum the reseller will be paid for selling your product, usually as a percentage of the sale price of the product. The agreement also addresses order processing, invoicing, and payment procedures.

A PDA works best when a business holds its own GSA Schedule and then uses multiple resellers to sell its products. A company holding a GSA Schedule can control its pricing and still retain the flexibility to strike deals with a number of resellers. Since each reseller your company works with may sell in a different federal market, the market for your products is greatly expanded. However, companies who work with multiple resellers often experience administrative headaches with respect to monitoring product pricing issues. Such headaches are nonexistent if your company is on a GSA Schedule and enters into a PDA with a reseller, since the prices are established by the Schedule and are the same for each reseller. In the event that your company enters into a PDA with a reseller, you must remember to modify your GSA Schedule contract to incorporate the PDA and the corresponding reseller into your Schedule.

Enter the term <u>GSA Participating Dealer</u> in the search engine of your choice to view some sample GSA Participating Dealer Agreements.

Letters of Supply and Commercial Sales Practice

For a variety of reasons, product vendors may choose to become suppliers to another company that holds a GSA Schedule contract. In such cases, GSA requires that the GSA Schedule holder—who in this instance would be a reseller—obtain a Letter of Supply (LOS) from the supplier when the reseller does not have enough sales history to have established prices in the commercial marketplace.

For example, say Company AGW manufactures widgets and has a Schedule contract allowing them to sell widgets and gizmos to the federal government. Company SLM also manufactures gizmos, but doesn't have a Schedule contract. AGW strikes a deal with SLM to sell their gizmos to the feds. AGW is then in effect a reseller, and will need to get a Letter of Supply from SLM to document established prices in the commercial marketplace.

Each GSA Schedule solicitation contains a Commercial Sales Practice section that outlines the data a supplier must provide to the reseller. The reseller then plugs that information into its GSA Schedule proposal. Prior to finalizing the GSA Schedule proposal, the reseller and supplier agree upon a price for each product and the reseller then marks up the agreed-upon prices to establish a final GSA offering price. The final markup is based on a number of factors, including the value added by the reseller, the GSA-approved prices for the same product on competitors' Schedules, and commercial sales practice data.

The decision to obtain your own GSA Schedule or sell through resellers under a Letter of Supply is not always simple. Some of the factors to consider are the tradeoff between the anticipated volume of potential sales under a GSA Schedule versus the associated administrative costs, the company's past federal sales history, and whether the more traditional sales channels used by the supplier have been successful.

Suppliers often opt to sell under Letters of Supply when:

- The supplier does not intend to sell directly to federal customers.

- The supplier is new to the market and does not want to make a large initial investment in obtaining and administering a GSA Schedule.

- The auditing standards and requirements for a supplier under a LOS are less onerous than those for a direct GSA Schedule holder. This can be particularly helpful to a small business just starting up.

- The company intends to sell to only a limited number of resellers.

If a business issues Letters of Supply to a large number of resellers, the administrative burden associated with monitoring pricing and other administrative issues under each Letter of Supply becomes too great. To reduce that burden, consider establishing a uniform pricing strategy with all of your resellers. A uniform strategy can be more easily maintained and controlled, and is consistent with the value added by the resellers. Other drawbacks to Letters of Supply include:

- The supplier must pay a commission to the reseller for any GSA sales made to a federal customer.

- The supplier loses a degree of control over the federal sales process.

- GSA pricing can be difficult to maintain; any price increases need to be negotiated with the contracting officer and do not always keep pace with real world pricing.

In summary, product suppliers new to the federal market may want to initially sell to resellers under Letters of Supply and then later consider obtaining their own GSA Schedule, depending on the number of resellers the company uses and the overall federal sales volume.

Riding Someone's Schedule: Teaming Agreements

To satisfy complex agency needs with a minimum of effort, federal buyers often seek "complete solutions" through a single purchase, rather than multiple buys. Because most companies can't do everything, they have to team up with other companies to satisfy such demands.

Teaming arrangements vary. Two or more Schedule contractors can seek Schedule work as a team. In such cases, each participating team member pays their share of the Industrial Funding Fee, and the teaming arrangement, including which company will serve as the team leader or prime contractor, is detailed in the contract. Alternatively, two or more companies form a partnership or joint venture to act as a potential prime contractor. A GSA Schedule holder could also bring in non-Schedule holders as subcontractors—this is commonly referred to as "riding someone's Schedule."

What are the potential benefits of teaming from the vendor's perspective? GSA lists the following pluses of a team agreement:

- Satisfies the customer with a single solution

- Increases competitive edge

- Increases market share

- Increases visibility

- Focuses on core capabilities

- Obtains complementary capabilities

- Integrates different skills

- Offers additional opportunities with customers

- Builds direct relationships with customers

- Maximizes use of one or more Schedule solutions

- Shares risks and rewards

- Increases small business participation

Structuring Teaming Deals

It is not within the purview of GSA to approve team arrangements; any contract arrangements are between the team members. The only real restriction is that the team agreement cannot conflict with the underlying terms and conditions of the GSA Federal Supply Schedule contract. Some common elements in teaming contracts identified by GSA include:

- Identifies participants, Schedules, and services and products covered by the arrangement and how additions/deletions will occur

- Defines terms

- Sets forth each participant's roles, responsibilities, and obligations

- Identifies scope, period of performance (for specific, limited purposes or longer periods covering several transactions), and termination of the arrangement

- Identifies remunerations for functions performed, if any

- Identifies the process that will be used to quote, accept, and administer orders. This may include prices, terms and conditions, invoicing, payment, taxes, reports, etc.

- Establishes scope and limitations of any licenses or proprietary rights

- Establishes representations and warranties among the parties

- Identifies confidentiality requirements, obligations, disclosures, and remedies

- Identifies damages, liability/limitation of liability, and any indemnification requirements among the parties

- Addresses administrative requirements (e.g., assignments, how notices will be conveyed and recognized, how changes or amendments will occur)

- Identifies any terms that survive the arrangement or termination

- Identifies governing laws, venues, etc.

- Establishes how disputes will be addressed and resolved

- Addresses force majeure, a clause included in contracts to remove liability for natural and unavoidable catastrophes that interrupt the expected course of events; you wouldn't have to keep paying rent on a warehouse in New Orleans that was wiped out by Katrina, despite having signed a rental agreement, for instance.

Forming a Team

So, when should you form a team? Form a team when procurements call for solutions that you can't meet all by yourself. A warehousing contract, for example, might require bar code equipment, software programming, logistics consulting, and a labor force hired to operate forklifts and pack boxes. Few, if any companies acting alone could meet all the requirements under such a contract.

With the right teaming arrangement, you can go after complex projects that would otherwise be beyond your capabilities. Take, for example, a large IT project requiring multiple types of products and expertise. A contractor with a GSA Schedule for integration services might form a joint venture with other Schedule holders who supply computer hardware, software, network operations, and maintenance services.

A teaming agreement should be drafted carefully, with due consideration given to such issues as proprietary information, the roles and responsibilities of each party, and contract duration. The firm designated as prime contractor would supervise the project, submit invoices, receive payment, manage the payroll, and assume overall responsibility for contract administration. In deciding which firm is the prime, team members should consider, among other things, which one is in the best position to generate government business for future projects.

GSA regulations state that an ordering agency's Request For Quotation requires vendors to specifically identify their teaming arrangements, designating "all team members, their corresponding GSA Schedule contract numbers, and describe the tasks to be performed by each team member, along with the associated proposed prices (e.g., unit prices, labor categories, and rates). If applicable, the team leader should also be identified."

Bottom line: Think Big. If you're on the Schedule but missing out on lucrative, complex opportunities, look around for the right teaming partners, so you can play with the big boys and girls.

A sample GSA teaming contract is included in Appendix E.

Blanket Purchase Agreements

Federal agencies can establish Blanket Purchasing Agreements (BPAs) under any GSA Schedule contract. A GSA Schedule BPA makes filling recurring needs for supplies or services simple, while leveraging a customer's buying power by taking advantage of quantity discounts, saving administrative time, and reducing paperwork.

In addition, the contractual terms and conditions contained in GSA Schedule contracts apply to GSA Schedule BPAs and therefore don't need to be renegotiated. This can eliminate contracting costs and the need to prepare and evaluate new solicitations. BPAs also:

- Provide an opportunity for the government to negotiate improved discounts based on volume purchases

- Reduce administrative efforts by eliminating repetitive, individual orders and payments

- Enable an ordering activity to use streamlined ordering procedures

- Permit an ordering activity to incorporate contractor teaming agreements

- Allow for quicker turnarounds on orders

A BPA can be set up for field offices across the nation, allowing them to place orders directly with GSA Schedule contractors. In doing so, the entire agency reaps the benefits of additional discounts negotiated under the BPA. A multi-agency BPA is also permitted if the BPA identifies the participating agencies and their estimated requirements at the time the BPA is established.

GSA's Blanket Purchase Agreement Frequently Asked Questions answers a variety of questions regarding the use of BPAs under GSA Schedule contracts. A Sample GSA Blanket Purchase Agreement is included in

Appendix F. Other information related to the use of BPAs can be found on the GSA website under:

- Establishment of BPAs

- Ordering From BPAs

- BPA Documentation

Chapter 8

Negotiating for Profit with GSA

Making a profit is the Holy Grail of most businesses. Negotiating pricing with GSA can be a remarkably trying experience. GSA always wants the best price you have ever given to anyone—GSA calls this Most Favored Customer prices—and then a little bit more.

GSA has a mandate to negotiate "fair and reasonable" prices from companies making an offer for a Schedule contract. The problem is that fair and reasonable is in the eye of the beholder. GSA determines whether a company's prices are fair and reasonable based on the prices and discounts the company offers to its commercial clients. The government's negotiating philosophy is that the open market determines fair and reasonable pricing.

This negotiating philosophy is a double-edged sword. On the up side, if your company has standard price lists, never offers discounts, charges high prices with a high profit margin, and has the invoices to back it all up, you're in a really good position to enter into negotiations with GSA.

If, on the other hand, you're a small company that has been working on federal contracts under the thumb of a prime contractor for the past several years, you face a monumental negotiating task. The prime has squeezed your labor rates down so low that thinking about your profit margin brings on an instant migraine. The prime is your only customer so your invoices show the low rates. Guess what happens when it comes time to negotiate with GSA? Those are the prices GSA wants to pay.

Or say you are a product company and you occasionally give large discounts to close deals in lean times. Obviously, your invoices show the low, deal-closing prices. Guess what prices GSA is going to be looking at during negotiations?

Standard Prices and Practices

GSA's expectation is that companies have a standard price list, whether it's published, or a strictly internal document, and then may or may not offer discounts to commercial, nonprofit, or government customers. Companies that price "to the market" can get a GSA schedule but they have to be prepared to offer the best price ever offered to anyone or present a strong justification of why GSA should not receive the best price.

Somewhat surprisingly, in our experience many companies do not have a standard price list. The biggest single problem most companies encounter when making a price proposal to GSA is defining precisely what their customer discounts are and the terms and conditions associated with each discount. Many companies do not follow formal, precisely defined rules in offering discounts. Many do it the "American way"—offering prices that will lead to closing any given deal at the time. We call this approach Seat of the Pants pricing.

A similar problem to not having standard price lists is not having standard discounting practices. Standard discounting practices are practices that your sales force follows without exception. Many companies' discounting practices are tied to closing a deal based on current market conditions. Just as is the case with establishing standard pricing, companies pursuing a Schedule contract are probably going to have to establish standard discounting practices and strictly adhere to these practices if awarded a GSA contract. In some cases, this may hurt the company or may not even be possible. In other cases, making the sales force adhere to a set discounting structure may benefit the company.

Companies without a standard price list have to create one retroactively to quantify their discounts. Worse yet these companies have to somehow justify the standard prices that they created to define their discounts. This is one of the biggest problems GSA Schedule applicants run into— defining discounts in a meaningful and understandable way and then relating these practices to the prices offered to the government.

GSA encourages companies to mirror their commercial pricing structures in their GSA price offers; but with deeper discounts for GSA, of course. For example, companies offering tiered pricing commercially (based on quantities purchased, dollar volumes, geography, etc.) should use the same tiers in their GSA offer, but with an added dollop of incentive for GSA.

However, GSA doesn't track cumulative order volume over time because orders can be placed by any federal agency anywhere in the world. Consequently, GSA doesn't negotiate discounts that go beyond a specific order level either within an agency or across agencies. For instance, you will not be talking about additional discounts when agency orders reach a level of $1,000,000.

Disclosing Discounting Practices

The biggest stumbling block for many companies is GSA's requirement to disclose your "Commercial Sales Practices." Companies new to the federal market often respond, "Do what?" GSA wants to know about any and all discounts your company has ever offered to any type of customer.

Always disclose your discounting practices no matter how deep the discount. During price negotiations with GSA, you can explain why a particular discount does not apply, using the argument that the terms and conditions of the discount are different from the terms and conditions of the solicitation. GSA holds most of the negotiating cards, but you can win this argument (occasionally) if the terms and conditions are wildly disparate and you make an articulately written and verbal case.

Failure to fully disclose discounting practices can result in downward price adjustments during the life of the contract, and the necessity for money being returned to GSA. It is an understatement to say that discount disclosures are the most critical part of a GSA proposal; they determine your GSA prices and your future audit risk.

GSA Pricing Definitions

GSA uses two terms that are central in price negotiation.

Most Favored Customer(s): The customer (or category of customer) offered your company's best price.

Basis of Award customer(s): The customer (or category of customer) and the discounts offered to this customer (or category of customer) that were used during price negotiations to establish the discounts offered to GSA. The Basis of Award customer could be a single customer (Company X), a small group of customers (your top three customers in terms of sales volume), or an entire category of customers (all corporate customers).

The price-negotiating wrestling match centers on these two concepts. The vendor submitting an offer to GSA usually identifies the Basis of Award customer or group of customers with a low discount and terms and conditions similar to those in the GSA Schedule solicitation. GSA usually seeks to make your Most Favored Customer the Basis of Award customer, even if the terms and conditions for your Most Favored Customer discounts are seriously different from the terms and conditions associated with the GSA solicitation.

The following example might clarify a company's dilemma.

Customer Category	Discounting Practice
Commercial customers	Customers purchasing less than $10,000 do not receive a discount
Commercial customers	Customers purchasing more than $10,000 in an individual order receive a 10% discount
Commercial customers	Customers purchasing more than $500,000 in an individual order receive a 25% discount

In the above example, a company's Most Favored Customers are commercial customers receiving discounts of 25% for purchasing more than $500,000 in an individual order.

GSA will argue in negotiations that the average order size under the Schedule contract will be in the $500,000 range. Assume that the company can convince GSA in their proposal and during negotiations that the average GSA order will be approximately $10,000. Then the Basis of Award would be commercial customers receiving discounts of 10% for purchasing more than $10,000 in an individual order.

The greater the disparity in order sizes, the easier it is to convince GSA on paper and in negotiations that the Basis of Award customer(s) should be the 10% customer group.

The order differential isn't usually as clear as the example above though, and the policies and instructions used by GSA in negotiating fair and reasonable prices are scattered throughout the GSA Schedule solicitation document. When you boil them down, the policies and instructions are somewhat subjective and open to a variety of interpretations.

Companies That Do Not Discount

Life is easier for companies that do not discount. The GSA solicitation essentially says:

- Show us your standard commercial price list (published or internal). If internal, provide invoices to justify your standard prices. If your price list is published, prove that anyone can see it either on the Internet or through a phone call.

- Certify that you do not discount, under penalties specified in the disclosure clause in the solicitation. (Frequently companies that initially think they don't discount reassess the situation when they learn of the disclosure clause.)

- Since you don't discount, GSA assumes that all your customers are both Most Favored Customers and Basis of Award customers; that is, all your customers receive standard prices.

- Now, the hooker. GSA still wants to negotiate and be offered prices better than your standard prices.

- As a reward for offering Most Favored Customer pricing (and then some), GSA will move your proposal through the evaluate/negotiate/award process quickly.

Discounters Offering Most Favored Customer Pricing

For companies that discount and are offering Most Favored Customer pricing, the GSA solicitation says:

- Show us your standard commercial price list (published or internal). If internal, provide invoices to prove your standard prices. If your price list is published, prove that anyone can see it either on the Internet or through a phone call.

- Answer the question: "Are you willing to offer GSA Most Favored Customer pricing—the best prices you have offered anyone?"

- If yes, disclose only your Most Favored Customer pricing. Your Most Favored Customer will be the Basis of Award customer.

- Now, let's negotiate. GSA still wants prices better than your Most Favored Customer pricing.

- As a reward for offering Most Favored Customer pricing, GSA will move your proposal through the evaluate/negotiate/award process quickly.

Discounters Not Offering Most Favored Customer Pricing

For companies that discount and are offering other than Most Favored Customer pricing the GSA solicitation says:

- Show us your standard commercial price list (published or internal). If internal, provide invoices to justify your standard prices. If your price list is published, prove that anyone can see it either on the Internet or through a phone call.

- Disclose all of your discounting practices; which by definition will disclose your Most Favored Customer pricing.

- Tell us which customer(s) receiving discounts have sale terms and conditions most like the terms and conditions of the solicitation. If we agree with the similarity of terms and conditions, this customer(s) will be the Basis of Award customer.

- If we don't agree, we will negotiate a Basis of Award customer(s), probably your Most Favored Customer.

- Now, what can you do for GSA? The government still wants prices better than those received by your Basis of Award customer.

- Be aware that your proposal may take longer to evaluate.

Although commercial companies may find the Schedule program frustrating, insensitive to market fluctuations, and flawed, ultimately it's a price-based system designed to maximize taxpayer value.

Price Reduction Clause

Why do we repeatedly stress the importance of scrupulously disclosing all of your discounting practices? Because GSA will reduce your Schedule prices retroactively if they discover inaccurate disclosure during a contract audit. Yes, all the way back to when the contract was first awarded, or when the inaccuracy occurred. The Price Reduction Clause is by far the most important clause in the solicitation and in your GSA Schedule contract. The clause reads:

> Before award of a contract, the Contracting Officer and the Offeror will agree upon (1) the customer (or category of customers) which will be the Basis of Award, and (2) the Government's price or discount relationship to the identified customer (or category of customers). This relationship shall be maintained throughout the contract period. Any change in the Contractor's commercial pricing or discount arrangement applicable to the identified customer (or category of customers) which disturbs this relationship shall constitute a price reduction.

> During the contract period, the Contractor shall report to the Contracting Officer all price reductions to the customer (or category of customers) that was the Basis of Award. The Contractor's report shall include an explanation of the conditions under which the reductions were made.

> You will be asked to submit a Final Proposal Revision Letter that states: (Name of Company) hereby agrees that the basis of negotiation for the Multiple Award Schedule for SIN xxxxx is predicated upon the following category of customer (Commercial End Users, National and Corporate Accounts, State and Local Governments, VARS, OEMS, Resellers/Dealers).

In plain English, the Price Reduction Clause says:

GSA negotiated a Basis of Award customer(s) with you. You specified in your proposal and during negotiations the discounts you give to your Basis of Award customer(s). GSA used these discounts to the specified customers to negotiate the prices in your contract. Your prices will be recalculated and money returned to GSA if you offer your Basis of Award customer(s) better discounts than those disclosed to GSA during contract negotiations.

The Price Reduction Clause ensures that your discounting practices and the GSA price are kept at a fixed relationship. If you provide a larger discount to a Basis of Award customer than what was agreed upon in your contract, your GSA price will go down proportionately and retroactively.

The "fixed relationship" is best described with an example. Say the discount to your Basis of Award customer(s) was 10%. You negotiated a discount with GSA for 12%. Two years into the contract, on December 1, 2007, one of your salespeople gave a discount to a Basis of Award customer of 15%—a 50% increase in the discount. That would raise your GSA discount to 18%, also effective December 1, 2007. GSA Schedule invoices will be recalculated—read reduced—as of December 1, 2007, and you will be required to pay GSA the total amount of the reduction. Ouch.

The good news is that the Price Reduction Clause is triggered only by sales to customers in your Basis of Award group of customers. Vendors can grant whatever discounts they want to commercial customers not included in the company's Basis of Award group without affecting the prices in the GSA Schedule contract.

You can see why negotiations defining the Basis of Award group are so crucial. Vendors generally want to select a very narrow Basis of Award group, while the government seeks as broad a Basis of Award as possible, so that virtually any discounted sale anywhere in the vendor's operations will entitle Schedule purchasers to comparable discounts. Thus the price-negotiating wrestling match.

Maximum Order Threshold

A Maximum Order Threshold (MOT) is specified in the GSA Request for a Proposal (RFP). The amount of the MOT is negotiable, and its significance is often missed. The key is that the Price Reduction Clause does not apply to orders exceeding the MOT. Thus, vendors seek the lowest possible MOT and GSA wants the amount of the MOT to be the amount specified in the solicitation.

The second reason that the MOT is important is that if an order exceeds a Schedule contract's maximum order threshold it automatically kicks in a federal purchasing rule requiring the buying agency to seek price reductions. The following information is published at gsa.gov.

> *While ordering activities are encouraged to seek price reductions for any size Schedule contract order, they are required to seek price reductions if a requirement exceeds a Schedule contract's maximum order threshold. The maximum order under a GSA Schedule contract is the dollar value threshold at which the ordering activity must seek additional price reductions for its requirement. The maximum order varies from contract to contract and is listed in every GSA Schedule contractor's pricelist and on GSA Advantage. In response to the ordering activity's request for a price reduction, the contractor may offer a lower price, offer the current Schedule contract price, or decline the order. If further price reductions are not offered, the order may still be placed if the ordering activity determines that it is appropriate, since GSA has already determined the contract prices to be fair and reasonable.*

GSA's position on requesting price reductions for orders below the Maximum Order Threshold is as follows:

> *Ordering activities are advised to seek further price reductions when requirements warrant. Price reductions allow ordering activities to take advantage of the flexible and dynamic pricing in the commercial marketplace. By requesting a price reduction, the ordering activity can maximize its use of GSA Schedule contracts by taking advantage of such factors as competitive forces, technological changes, labor conditions, supply and demand, industry sales goals, and inventory reductions.*

> *Reasons to seek price reductions include instances where the ordering activity has determined that a supply or service is available elsewhere at a lower price, or when establishing Blanket Purchase Agreements (BPAs) to fill recurring requirements. The potential volume of orders under BPAs offers the opportunity to secure price reductions/increased discounts, regardless of the size of individual orders. Ordering activities should also seek price reductions when the annual review of a BPA reveals that estimated quantities/amounts have been exceeded.*

You probably won't be surprised to learn that you can offer lower prices to agencies buying under GSA Schedules without triggering the Price Reduction Clause.

The Ties That Bind

A GSA proposal is a monstrous document full of red tape. And yet when you cut through all the legwork—the information gathering, writing, exhibit preparation, document formatting, the seemingly endless questions that have to be answered …… it all comes down to one thing: Establishing your contract pricing. And negotiating pricing with GSA poses a dilemma for many companies.

Discounting practices and proposed GSA prices are inextricably tied to each other. The single biggest problem companies experience in making an offer to GSA is not tying the two together truthfully for fear that it will result in a lower price. Don't make this mistake. GSA will insist that you disclose all discounts and then base your price on your discounts. Get it right, up front in the original proposal, because you will have to in the end or not receive a contract award.

Life would be wonderful if you could just say to GSA: "Our standard price list is enclosed and let's forget about those occasional 30% discounts we grant now and then to make our numbers."

Unfortunately, that's not the way it is.

Chapter 9

Price Negotiation

You will negotiate prices more effectively with GSA if you understand the dilemma contracting officers face. GSA wants to award GSA Schedule contracts. At the same time, the contracting officers are charged with obtaining the lowest prices possible, protecting the interests of the taxpayer, and are subject to the scrutiny of auditors and Congress. This push-pull of these essentially conflicting mandates can make arriving at competitive and yet profitable pricing a negotiating nightmare, and GSA negotiators can begin to appear quite bull-headed and unreasonable to you.

A defensible paper trail documenting that the negotiated prices are fair and reasonable is the Holy Grail of a GSA contracting officer. Understand this and help build a rational case for your pricing. Although price negotiations are inherently adversarial, GSA has most of the cards. Companies that attempt to "take them on" usually lose. So do your best to work with them in building a case for your prices.

Negotiating with GSA

Even though it may sometimes feel like a one-way street, price negotiation with GSA is just that, a negotiation. The one-way street feeling stems from the knowledge that GSA is in fact in the power position.

Think of it this way. Imagine that you (as GSA) are buying a car and you could demand the following from a car dealer.

"I would like to see, on paper, all of the discounts from sticker price that you (the car dealer) have offered in the past year. Now, give me the lowest price you have given to anyone. And you will have to agree to adjust the price downward if I find out later that you did not disclose certain discounts or that you are giving lower prices than you disclosed on paper.

And, by the way, I am not buying right now and can't guarantee any orders. But I may want thousands of cars in the future so let's set a price based on your biggest discount in case I do buy from you."

And so the haggling begins. The dealer counters by saying that the 20% off sticker was for 100 cars in a single order to the same place, unlike the buyer's situation, who might purchase a few cars destined for random places sometime in the distant future. So locking in a big discount is inappropriate in this situation. The buyer responds that it is the world's biggest customer and could potentially buy thousands of cars.

The GSA negotiation process is similar to the scenario described above.

Here's an alternative scenario. You disclosed in your GSA proposal: "We give Customer A a 40% discount. However, Customer A is a long-standing, high volume customer. They make more than 50% of the purchases from our business and they continue to order with almost no sales costs. We would go bankrupt if we offered 40% to GSA."

There would still be some haggling, but in this (admittedly extreme) example, you would have a shot at convincing GSA that the government discount should be less than that of your Most Favored customer. In reality, most cases are not this clear cut.

Best and Worst Case Scenarios

So what kinds of companies do best in the price-based GSA negotiation process?

- Companies that have standard, stable prices and do not discount
- Companies that have standard, stable prices and do discount but have strict, volume based discounting practices
- Companies that have federal customers with established, profitable prices specified in federal contracts
- And what kinds of companies have trouble in negotiating with GSA.
- Companies with wide-ranging and uncertain discounting practices
- Companies that have fluctuating prices

- Companies that discount according to market conditions

- Companies with low hourly rates resulting from working as subcontractors under federal prime contracts

GSA Pricing Policies

Over the past several years, GSA's emphasis on obtaining the lowest possible price when negotiating GSA Schedule contracts has been spurred by fear of auditors second- guessing them.

The following is a paragraph from the Schedule 00CORP Consolidated Schedule Request for Proposal, which applies to contractors who provide two or more combined Schedule services, such as facilities maintenance, human resources, training, information technology, and financial and business solutions. Note the reference to the General Accounting Office.

> ***Pricing goal: Most Favored Customer (MFC)****: The GSA Federal Supply Service awards over $5 billion dollars annually for goods and services under the Schedules program; one of the largest single contracting activities in the nation. GSA has a fiduciary responsibility to the American taxpayers and to customer agencies to take full advantage of the Government's leverage in the market in order to obtain the best deal for the taxpayer. Accordingly, the U.S. General Accounting Office has specifically recommended that "the price analysis GSA does to establish the Government's Multiple Award Schedule (MAS) negotiation objective should start with the best discount given to any of the vendor's customers." GSA seeks to obtain the offeror's best (i.e., MFC) price based on its evaluation of discounts, terms, conditions, and concessions offered to commercial customers. Offerors inquire frequently as to a means of facilitating the processing of their contract offers. There are many factors involved, but all things being equal, an initial MFC offer requires less review and analysis and is therefore more likely to be finalized rapidly.*

This policy could easily be interpreted as saying: "Cave in and give the government Most Favored Customer pricing even though it is not particularly profitable because you will get your Schedule faster."

Judging "Fair and Reasonable"

The federal acquisition regulations say that GSA should seek to negotiate a fair and reasonable price and that the terms and conditions of a company's discounting practices should be considered in determining what is fair and reasonable. The regulations state that the commercial terms and conditions of a company's discounts may be different from the terms and conditions of GSA Schedule contracts. For instance, Company JLW buys 10,000 cars a year, all delivered to Toledo; Ohio. The government plans to buy 20 cars and wants them delivered to 20 different places. These differences may result in GSA prices that are higher than prices offered to a company's Most Favored Customer.

Under the "fair and reasonable" directive, contracting officers should compare the terms and conditions of the vendor's commercial sales to the terms and conditions of the GSA Schedule contract, and use his or her best judgment in determining a fair and reasonable price for the offered product or service.

Despite the fact that federal regulations clearly state that there may be a reason that the government is not entitled to Most Favored Customer pricing, contracting officers are frequently uncomfortable exercising this kind of judgment, particularly if there are auditors hovering over them. Auditors, in turn, are noted for viewing issues as either black or white. Subjective decisions, even when rational, create the opportunity to be second-guessed and, not surprisingly contracting officers are leery of leaving themselves open to such criticism.

Adversarial Negotiating in the Name of the Taxpayer

Discounting is a way of life for most companies, particularly those selling products as opposed to services. For many industries, it's the only way to survive, and GSA regulations recognize this. But when negotiating, GSA is an adversary. Be prepared to answer the following questions in your proposal and during verbal price negotiations.

- Why shouldn't we receive your very best discount or even more? We are the world's biggest customer.

- Are the terms and conditions extended to your best customers different from those in the solicitation?

- Will you extend the best customer terms and conditions to us?

Companies frequently ask why GSA is so inflexible in demanding Most Favored Customer pricing. The answer is they don't have to be flexible, and from the viewpoint of the taxpayer, maybe they shouldn't be. In addition, the threat of auditors, Congressional investigations, and media exposés always linger in the back of the contracting officer's mind.

Yet GSA does understand clear-cut cases and is flexible if a strong case can be made for less than Most Favored Customer pricing. It is the wishful thinking cases and grey areas where the GSA contracting office becomes rigid.

Money Losers

Vendors who simply cannot offer GSA their Most Favored Customer pricing without losing money face a quandary. Unfortunately, there isn't a good answer to this problem.

We suggest building as strong an argument as possible in your price proposal. When challenged by GSA, stick to your guns and be prepared to fight the fight. You will win or lose based on the documentation you can provide that the prices you are offering are fair and reasonable. The operative words in the regulations are "may" and "consider." The bottom line is that GSA can in fact demand Most Favored Customer pricing if the contracting officer feels that it is in the best interest of the taxpayer. The government has the upper hand and it's up to you to convince GSA of your case.

The Negotiation Process

Keep the following in mind when negotiating GSA Schedule prices.

You are negotiating with a person, not a bureaucracy. The GSA contracting officer or contract specialist may be experienced and reasonable, inexperienced and unreasonable, or anything in between. Yet they all want to approve contracts based on a documented file that shows that the taxpayer is receiving a fair and reasonable price.

Don't rush negotiations. Document your arguments by email, and patiently work with the contracting officer or contracting specialist to build a file that demonstrates that your price is fair and reasonable. The operative words here are "work with." Working with contracting officers in a frank and open manner is essential to success in the federal market. They are not out to beat you up; it's in their best interest as well as yours to establish a productive working partnership.

Want to get it done quickly without haggling? Offer your Most Favored Customer pricing in your initial proposal. Many companies can and do offer Most Favored Customer pricing up front. GSA will process proposals offering Most Favored Customer pricing ahead of those that don't.

Countering the "World's Biggest Customer" Argument

The problem most companies face when trying to argue that GSA's prices should be higher than your Most Favored Customer is that GSA will almost always say: "We are the world's biggest customer, and we should have better than your best price even if the terms and conditions vary."

The "world's biggest customer" argument may apply to a large prime contractor with thousands of established federal relationships. It's up to you to convince GSA that it does not apply to a small business new to the market.

To the small business owner, GSA may in fact be the world's most expensive market. The market is spread across thousands of agencies worldwide. Finding and selling end-users in individual federal agencies requires significant business development and sales costs, and there can be a long lag time between submitting a proposal and making a profit. The cost of making individual GSA sales may far exceed the average cost of a commercial sale.

Don't be shy; bring these points up in your proposal and during verbal price negotiations. GSA regulations say that the contracting officers should listen and be open to the unique circumstances of small businesses. Whether a given contracting officer buys your argument is sometimes just a roll of the dice.

Negotiating as a Market-Based Discounter

Companies that discount based on market conditions—i.e. indiscriminate discounting—face a difficult path when negotiating with GSA. The GSA pricing policies are based on the principle of set price and discounting practices. The exact opposite philosophy drives market conditions discounting.

For instance, say Company AGW manufactures plywood. Some years are good, others, not so much, and plywood prices go up and down, but within a reasonable range. One year the company execs bank on hurricane forecasts predicting a horrendous hurricane season and the company manufactures massive quantities of plywood. At the end of a markedly mild hurricane season, the company is disastrously over-stocked and sells the plywood at an eyelash above cost. GSA will begin negotiations asking for a discount equal to or greater than Company AGW's largest discount.

One way to solve the problem is to tell GSA that your company is establishing set discounting policies and then negotiate a reasonable GSA price based on an agreement with GSA not to exceed a set discount. However, you will actually have to discontinue indiscriminate discounting and not exceed the agreed upon discount or you will trigger the dreaded Price Reduction Clause.

Many companies either can't or won't establish set discounting policies. We often have people leave our GSA proposal workshops saying that establishing set discounting practices in their businesses is long overdue and would probably improve the bottom line in the long run. A favorite refrain is "Maybe this will finally get the owners to stop playing the pricing game by the seat of their pants."

Keep in mind: If you say you are going to stop sinning—being an indiscriminant market discounter—in your proposal, then you better actually adhere to the stated discounting policy or the GSA auditors will surely dole out the penance.

Other possible solutions:

- Accept a discount equal to or greater than your Most Favored Customer. (And in the case of Company AGW, go bankrupt.)

- Ask GSA to disregard the most extreme discounts using a terms and conditions argument and settle on a GSA discount based on ranges or averages of your market discounts. This is a very difficult argument to make under current policies at GSA because indiscriminate discounts are usually not based on terms and conditions.

Chapter 10

Discounting Practices and the Commercial Sales Practice Format

GSA solicitations require that you disclose your company's discounting practices. Known as the Commercial Sales Practices Format (CSP), this can be one of the most confusing and stickiest aspects of doing business with the federal government.

CSPs vary slightly by solicitation. For example, the CSP Format for the Schedule 70 General Purpose Commercial Information Technology Equipment, Software, and Services Solicitation, is included in Appendix E. Steps to take to complete a CSP include:

Step 1 Determine the GSA Discount

Many companies prepare bids designed to address unique customer specifications. Service companies then have to quantify the unit prices used to prepare the bids: hourly rates, per square foot rates, and so on. This can be complicated when unit price varies by geographic region and blue collar service wages are dictated by state and federal legislation.

Products companies usually solve the per bid pricing dilemma by defining a base model with options. Then they have the problem of justifying the base and options prices through invoices.

GSA is flexible in that they allow companies to model their commercial pricing structure in their GSA price proposal, e.g., unit pricing schemes, volume discounting structures, etc., provided that the pricing models are well defined and followed in practice. For example, companies with regional pricing due to geographic cost disparities can offer prices by region. Companies offering volume discounts for purchase of set quantities or dollar amounts can offer discounts by quantity or dollar volume.

Step 2 Define Your Best Customer

The next step is to answer the question "Are our proposed GSA discounts equal to or better than the best price offered to any customer acquiring the same items regardless of quantity or terms and conditions?" If the answer to this question is yes, you only have to disclose in the Commercial Sales Practices Format those discounts offered to your best customer. Answering yes simplifies your GSA proposal and speeds up the evaluation process at GSA.

If the answer to the question above is "no," you must disclose in the Commercial Sales Practices Format all of your discounting practices currently in effect. You must then convince GSA in your pricing proposal why you believe that your best discount should not be granted to GSA.

Product Price Proposal

The price proposal formats required by GSA vary from schedule to schedule. They do, however, have common elements. The following example shows a GSA price proposal for a single product priced commercially at $100. Discounting practice assumptions and proposed GSA pricing for the example are as follows.

Discounting Practices: Commercial customers purchasing more than $10,000 in an individual order receive a 10% discount

If the discounting practice is not strictly followed, any exceptions would have to be disclosed in the company's proposal.

Most Favored Customer: Commercial Customers Purchasing More than $10,000 in an Individual Order

Basis of Award Customer: All Commercial Customers

Product Number	Commercial Price	GSA Price	GSA Discount	GSA Price Including Shipping (1)	GSA Discount Including 0.75 % Industrial Funding Fee (2)
12345	$100	$90	10%	$99	$99.74

(1) Average shipping cost: 10% (GSA will require justification for this cost.)

(2) GSA Price Including Shipping × 0.75 (Adds back the Industrial Funding Fee.)

In this example, the company had a single discounting practice for the product and followed the practice without exception. The Most Favored Customer price and the proposed GSA price are the same.

The company is therefore offering GSA Most Favored Customer pricing and the Basis of Award Customer becomes "All Commercial Customers". This presumes that GSA would accept Most Favored Customer pricing without a further discount. This probably is not a good assumption in today's GSA environment.

"All Commercial Customers" would become the Basis of Award Customer named in the GSA contract. Presuming that GSA accepts the proposed pricing, the company's GSA price would be adjusted downward if the company gives discounts of greater than 10% to any commercial customer.

Although simplistic, the example of a single $100 product illustrates the basic principles of presenting a proposed price to GSA. A spreadsheet presenting a line of products or separate spreadsheets (or Word tables) can be used to show price offers for products with different discounting practices and different proposed GSA discounts.

In the example, the commercial price is used as a standard for calculating the GSA discount. For most GSA Schedule solicitations, shipping costs must be included in the final GSA price. The method for calculating shipping costs must be presented to GSA and justified as part of the price proposal.

Normally, GSA accepts increasing a product price by the amount of the Industrial Funding Fee (IFF), because it is a cost required by the GSA contract. Recently some GSA evaluators have shown more reluctance to accept a 0.75% increase in the proposed price to offset the required IFF cost. The issue is negotiable.

Service Price Proposal

The following example shows a GSA price proposal for a service priced commercially at $100 per hour. Discounting practice assumptions and proposed GSA pricing for the example are as follows:

Discounting Practices: Commercial customers receive discounts of up to 10% for large projects (large is not specifically quantified by the company)

Most Favored Customer: Commercial Customers Receiving Discounts of up to 10%

Basis of Award Customer: All Commercial Customers

Labor Category	Commercial Price (per hour)	GSA Price (per hour)	GSA Discount	GSA price Including 0.75% Industrial Funding Fee
Senior Engineer	$100/hr	$90/hr	10%	$90.68

In this example, the company has a single discounting practice for the service, followed the practice without exception, and was willing to offer GSA Most Favored Customer pricing. Any exceptions to the single discounting practice would have to be disclosed in the company's proposal if the practice is not strictly followed.

The proposed GSA price is the company's Most Favored Customer price. The Basis of Award customer proposed to GSA was "All Commercial Customers". In other words, the Basis of Award price and the Most Favored Customer Price are the same. "All Commercial Customers" would become the Basis of Award customer named in the GSA contract.

Then any discounts greater than 10% to any commercial customer would trigger a GSA price reduction.

Although simplistic, the example of a single labor category priced at $100 per hour illustrates the basic principles of presenting a proposed price to GSA. Separate tables would show price offers for services with different discounting practices and different proposed GSA discounts.

Price Increases for Products

Generally, product price increases are limited as follows:

- Only three increases will be considered during each five-year contract period. Increases must be requested after the first 30 days of the contract period and prior to the last 60 days of the contract period.

- At least 30 days must elapse between requested increases.

- The aggregate of the increases in any contract unit price cannot exceed a pre-established percentage of the initial GSA contract price. This percentage will normally be 10%, unless trends—as measured by an appropriate index like the Producer Price Index—suggest otherwise. The contracting officer must approve a percentage greater than 10%. GSA reserves the right to raise this ceiling when changes in market conditions during the contract period support an increase.

You should consider seeking different terms for price adjustments or reconsider offering selected products if your products are historically characterized by rising list prices. GSA will consider different price increase terms if a strong case can be made as part of your GSA proposal. You should negotiate special price increase terms before your GSA contract is awarded.

Price Increases for Services

Price increases for services may be requested (or automatically become effective) on or after the first 12 months of the contract period. GSA will consider two arguments for price increases:

- Adjustments based on escalation rates are negotiated prior to contract award. Usually, the negotiations result in fixed annual increases in rates that become part of your contract and are effective on the 12-month anniversary dates of the contract. Currently, negotiated increases are limited to an annual ceiling of 4%. Although allowed, this method is no longer used by most GSA contracting officers.

- Annual adjustments based on an agreed-upon market indicator prior to award. The market indicator is usually a public index, public survey, or other public-based market indicator. This method appears to be the preferred method most GSA contracting officers are now using. Currently, the index most frequently used by GSA for professional services contracts is the Department of Labor's Employment Cost Index for Professional, Technical, and Specialty Workers, Table 3.

GSA also recognizes the potential impact of unforeseeable major changes in market conditions. When changes occur, the contracting officer will review requests to make adjustments, subject to the government's examination of industry-wide market conditions.

The Heart of Negotiations

At its heart, negotiating profitable GSA Schedule prices is a sales process. You must convince GSA in your proposal and with documented price refinements during negotiations that the prices you are offering are fair and reasonable in relation to the prices you are currently offering to others. Make a strong and convincing case based on full disclosure of discounting practices and you will probably end up with fair and reasonable prices. Hide reality or present a sloppy case on paper and you will lose. Remember, auditors and Congressional watchdogs are a constant concern for GSA contracting officers. Work with GSA to document your price justification rationale and you will find them reasonable.

Chapter 11

GSA Audits

Companies new to the federal market are frequently mystified by GSA Schedule audits and fear them, just as many people fear IRS audits. In both cases, a lot of the fear stems from not understanding the reason for the audit, or the potential exposure to adverse findings.

Companies submitting their first proposals for government sales frequently ask us why GSA insists on the right to audit when their commercial customers don't. Reason Number One is that GSA requires audit rights because they can. The right to pre-audit a company making an offer to the federal government is specifically spelled out in GSA Schedule solicitations.

GSA bases Schedule prices on your commercial prices, and assumes that the market makes your prices fair and reasonable. If a company gives commercial discounts, GSA negotiates prices based on those discounts, and requires that no bigger discounts be given to commercial customers. So the second reason for auditing is to ensure that GSA continues to receive the best price you offer.

What Should You Fear (if anything)?

Everyone fears audits; it's natural to fear unknown outcomes. Most government audits don't result in severe consequences—as long as you didn't deliberately set out to deceive the government. An IRS auditor may ding you for your home office expense deductions but that usually will not break the bank. On the other hand, the ding for failing to report income is could result in the sound of prison doors slamming shut.

It's the same with GSA audits. Unintentional violations will probably result in a ding; intentional pricing violations can result in big dollars going in the wrong direction. GSA may exact penalties for minor cases of excessive pricing on open market items—the random copier machine purchased under a Schedule contract for Airborne Radio and Television Communication Equipment, for instance.

The real problems come with violations of the Price Reduction clause, which will result in a downward adjustment of pricing way back to when the violation occurred. That could cost you a lot of money. You do not want to get caught with your discounting practices pants down.

Justifiable Fear

Needless to say, outright criminal fraud is also not a good thing to have revealed in an audit. In cases of demonstrable deceit, GSA could seek damages under the False Claims Act. Deceit would probably fall into two categories: (1) knowingly submitting false information in your GSA proposal and during price negotiations, and (2) giving discounts that you promised GSA you wouldn't.

Should you fear forgetting to disclose a large discount? It depends on whether the omission was a mistake or purposeful—and the burden of proof is on you. Most auditors will start out assuming purposeful deception (guilty until proven innocent), but a lot depends on the type and impact of the non-disclosure.

In cases of serious fraud, you could face both civil and criminal penalties, including treble damages, contract cancellation, and debarment from any future government work. Obviously, you would need a lawyer in a situation involving fraud.

Keep in mind, the federal government is not out to do you in. Although deplorable, sloppy bookkeeping practices, ineptitude, or even downright stupidity are different from actual criminal intent to defraud the government. If you've kept your hands clean, audit fear should not keep you up at night.

The Big Threat

The fire-eating dragon of audit threats is violation of the Price Reduction Clause (PRC). As discussed earlier, this type of violation occurs when a company offers a commercial customer in your Basis of Award group a higher discount than what you negotiated with GSA, and then not notifying your contract officer.

The GSA audit uncovers the new discounting practice for the Basis of Award group and GSA recalculates all your invoices based on the proportionately larger discount all the way back to when the violation occurred, and collects the adjusted amount in a lump sum.

Single refunds to the government in the $100 million dollar range have occured. GSA has collected refunds of this magnitude from large information technology contractors for price violations that occurred over many years.

Although rare, these cases do illustrate the seriousness of PRC violations. Obviously, this is a threat that should keep you up at night if you suspect that your company has violated the PRC.

Although far less menacing than the PRC violation, there are several other problems that could prove troublesome in an audit.

- Offering products from countries other than Designated Countries listed in the Trade Agreement Act. North Korea, China, and Taiwan fall under this category. Designated countries are our friends and trading partners. Countries not listed are "bad countries" or countries we don't like politically.

- Selling open market items as part of a GSA Schedule order without designating them as open market. An open market item is an item not listed on a company's GSA Schedule.

- Not accounting for and paying the Industrial Funding Fee correctly

- Inadequate invoicing and contract administration procedures

- Work performed and billed to the government that was not within the scope of the GSA contract. The example most often cited is prisoner interrogation services at the Abu Ghraib prison in Iraq, procured under a contract for Information Technology services. As you might guess, prisoner interrogation is not listed as a service on any GSA Schedule.

Guard against these threats through the implementation of an effective internal tracking and accounting system.

Types of Audits

GSA conducts two types of audits—pre-award and post-award. The scope and thoroughness of the two audits varies with the amount of revenue generated by a contract, and the complexity of the contract's pricing structure.

Although rare, GSA occasionally conducts an audit prior to the award of a new contract. The focus of a pre-award audit is to verify disclosures regarding commercial sales discounting practices and to determine whether the accounting systems in place can accurately track sales and compute the Industrial Funding Fee (IFF).

Pre-award audits are more typically conducted prior to GSA approval of a contract extension for an option period. An audit conducted prior to the approval of a 5-year option renewal will look at pricing and invoicing records for the current contract period as well as discounting disclosures and proposed pricing for the upcoming 5-year option period.

If you hold a GSA contract that generates a large number of sales, you're likely to be audited before a 5-year option is exercised. Contracts with small sales may never be audited. Then again, you never know. Although rare, post-award audits can occur at any time while a contract is active. They can be conducted to verify:

- Compliance with the Price Reduction Clause

- Correct payment of IFF

- Accuracy of billing

- Compliance with open market item designation requirements

- Proper invoicing of other direct charges

- Compliance with Trade Agreement Act regulations

What Triggers a GSA Audit?

Like an IRS audit, you never know what might trigger a GSA audit. Obviously, a current or former employee alleging a contract violation could trigger a post-award audit. In such a case the audit would focus entirely on the current contract period and not the upcoming option period. Other possible triggers that could increase the probability of an audit include:

- Your proposal for renewal of a 5-year option period indicates potential pricing problems.

- You are generating a lot of sales of products or professional services—GSA focuses its audits on where the action is.

- Your contract file at GSA has holes in it, or your contracting officer suspects that your contract administration is less than stellar.

- A visit by a GSA Industrial Operations Analyst to review your IFF payment record indicates potential contract problems.

- Your pricing and discounting practices were not straightforward in your original proposal. For instance, your pricing structure is based on cost rather than on the prices you charge commercial companies.

- Your company was acquired or you acquired another company.

- A red flag has been raised concerning scope of work of orders, excessive ordering of open market items, purchases of products from countries other than those designated in the Trade Agreement Act, or there have been specific violations prevalent in your industry.

The IFF Trigger

The Industrial Funding Fee (IFF) is a fee—0.75% on most contracts, 0.50% on medical contracts—paid by the contractor for every transaction conducted under a GSA Schedule. The fee covers GSA negotiating and contract administration services.

The IFF is the fuel that keeps the bureaucratic fire burning brightly. GSA employees love it because it pays their salaries. Companies have been known to try to avoid paying the IFF. GSA can be very aggressive in its quest for the fee, particularly during pre- and post-award reviews by Industrial Operations Analysts (IOA).

The IOA focuses on the IFF reporting and payment processes. An IOA visit should not be construed as a full-blown audit—the GSA Office of the Inspector General (OIG) conducts those. OIG audits can scrutinize all aspects of contract compliance in varying degrees of detail and scope depending on what triggered the audit. IOA visits to make sure that each new Schedule holder understands the absolute necessity of paying the IFF on time.

Protecting Yourself from Adverse Audit Consequences

Implementing an internal GSA compliance system is the only foolproof way to protect against adverse audit consequences. An effective GSA compliance system is not difficult to establish. Simply follow basic management principles—designate clear lines of authority and accountability, and measure performance against a specific standard.

A compliance system will protect you if it begins with your initial proposal and uses full disclosure as a basis for compliance over the term of the contract. Although not ideal, a compliance system implemented after contract award can bring a contract into compliance, although sometimes at the expense of profits.

The basic premises behind an effective GSA Compliance System are:

- Disclose discounting practices completely and accurately in your initial proposal. If you are implementing a system in the middle of a contract period, correct any inaccuracies that turn up immediately, and let your contracting officer know about them.

- Appoint a senior person in your financial organization as the GSA Compliance Officer.

- Communicate any possible compliance violation issues in writing to the GSA contracting officer immediately upon detection. Propose swift and practical corrective actions and request guidance and approval of your actions from the contracting officer.

Desire to Comply

This may sound obvious, but an effective compliance system begins with a company's desire to comply. Some companies don't really want to be utterly straightforward about their discounting policies because of the loss of flexibility in discounting to non-GSA customers. (Yes, compliance can affect sales in some cases.)

Yet you cannot afford to be anything but absolutely scrupulous in adhering to the conditions of your GSA contract because of the dangers of invoking the Price Reduction Clause. In many cases forcing discounting discipline can actually be a good thing. Sales might go down slightly but profits go up. Play the discounting game loosely and you may win or you may lose. If you lose, you will usually lose big.

Put Someone in Charge

Designate a single person in your financial organization as the GSA Compliance Officer. Whether full or part time, the person must have the authority to ensure GSA contract compliance and be accountable for making the company compliant. In order of importance, the responsibilities of the GSA Compliance Officer should be to:

- Document and enforce the discounting policies used to establish the GSA Basis of Award pricing structure.

- Design and enforce compliance procedures that outline the consequences for discounting violations committed by the sales staff. For example, monetary penalties could be imposed for one-time violators; repeat offenders might face termination. Obtain CEO approval of the compliance policies and procedures.

- Train sales staff and management in all aspects of GSA compliance.

- Monitor Basis of Award customer quotes and orders for compliance.

- Ensure the accuracy and payment of the quarterly Industrial Funding Fee to GSA on time. (GSA will love you for this one.)

- Monitor Trade Agreement Act compliance.

- Review each GSA order for excessive or unmarked open market items and out-of-scope work or products.

Most importantly, your company's GSA compliance officer should establish an open and ongoing relationship with the GSA contracting officer. Contract problems and proposed solutions should be communicated in writing and by telephone as soon as they are discovered. The two parties should establish a relationship based on trust and a commonly held view that your company and the government are partners.

This is the real secret of contract compliance. Experienced federal contractors know this, which is one of the reasons they get bigger and bigger.

Implementing a Compliance Program

Systems and procedures should be put in place to segregate GSA orders from those placed by your commercial customers. This will help support the reporting efforts of both your company's GSA compliance officer and any GSA auditor that shows up on your doorstep. As mentioned earlier, GSA loves two things:

1.   Collecting the Industrial Funding Fee—the more the better, and

2.   Seeing segregated GSA orders in your accounting system.

GSA order segregation enhances your ability to calculate the IFF correctly and pay it on time, and enables GSA to verify contract compliance easily and quickly.

Order segregation can take many forms, depending on your company's accounting system and the amount of GSA business you do. Creating a field in your accounting system for the GSA contract number is ideal because it allows for order segregation if you hold more than one GSA contract. A spreadsheet for GSA orders tied to the accounting system by your internal order number can be just as effective for smaller companies or companies with relatively inflexible accounting systems.

You should also implement paper or electronic procedures that allow your company's GSA compliance officer to monitor any discounted price quotes being offered to your Basis of Award customers to ensure contract compliance both before and after contract award.

Obviously, preventing violations by maintaining the capability to monitor discounting sales offers before-the-fact is better than discovering violations after-the-fact.

Again, after-the-fact compliance violations should be reported to the GSA contracting officer as soon as they are found. This will allow you to either adjust the prices you're charging GSA now, or (if you're really lucky) to correct the problem, with the contracting officer's approval, without incurring a price reduction. In either case, it beats owing a multi-million dollar refund to GSA down the line. Boards of Directors hate surprises.

The Three Cs of GSA Contract Management

The three Cs of effective GSA contract management and administration are Compliance, Communication, Common Sense. GSA contract administration is not complex. Know what the contract says. Do what it says and don't play discounting games. Make accurate discounting disclosures, monitor the Basis of Award group for any price reductions, and pay the Industrial Funding Fee on time. Don't cut corners. If you discover problems, correct them immediately and communicate the problem and corrective action taken with the contracting officer.

Play it straight with GSA and you will have nothing to fear. You will never achieve compliance if you decide to play a non-disclosure game with GSA to maximize your GSA prices. You may not be audited but you will toss and turn at night, plagued by the mega-GSA Price Refund or lawsuit bogeyman.

Chapter 12

Making an Offer to GSA

Unlike contracts put out for bid by the federal government using a standard Request for Proposal process that has a clearly defined bidding period, vendors can submit a proposal for a GSA Schedule contract at any time, and can always resubmit a proposal for reconsideration if the initial proposal is rejected. These two attributes are what make GSA Schedule contracts so attractive to small- and medium-sized businesses. We call the two key aspects "Open to all" and "It's Never Over."

The process for obtaining a GSA Schedule contract is as follows:

1.   The government publishes GSA Schedule solicitations on the Internet at Federal Business Opportunities (FedBizOpps), www.fedbizopps.gov.

2.   A vendor wanting to sell to the federal government prepares a proposal and submits it to GSA.

3.   GSA evaluates the vendor's offer.

4.   Contracting officers, with the assistance of contracting specialists, will ask the vendor to submit additional information. Some degree of proposal refinement is almost always required because of the complexity of the solicitation documents and the subjectivity of the proposal evaluation process.

5.   Using information submitted by the vendor, GSA contracting officers identify the vendor's best customers and prepare for negotiations.

6.   Negotiations are conducted.

7. Price proposal revisions are submitted.

8. A contract is either awarded for a 5-year period or the offer is rejected.

9. Contractors awarded a Schedule contract are required to prepare and distribute an "Authorized Federal Supply Schedule Price List."

10. GSA prints Federal Supply Schedule price lists for newly awarded contracts that are distributed to buyers through the Centralized Mailing List Service (CMLS). This is in theory. One of the complaints new contractors often voice is that they never see this list.

11. Contractors must post their pricing information electronically on GSA Advantage!, the government's e-mall. Contracting officers approve electronic submissions.

Defining Discounting: Are There Any Answers Out There?

For many, the idea of writing a proposal for a GSA Schedule contract ranks just short of "I'd rather stick my hand in a fire. Both hands. Up to the elbows."

Why are GSA Schedule proposals so difficult to write? Why is the back and forth of proposal refinement, rejection, and more refinement so extended and excruciating? Why is the GSA price evaluation process less than perfect? Why aren't there answers to the multitude of questions about Schedules?

The answer to all of these questions is the same. The GSA Schedule offer/evaluation/negotiation process is based on a company's commercial pricing and discounting practices. In theory, this seems simple and straightforward. However, most companies start out asking the most fundamental question:

"What's a discounting practice? We sell at the prices the market will bear. To survive in our market you do what you have to do to make a deal."

Many small- to medium-sized companies don't have standard price lists, never mind standard discounting practices. So the reality is that using a company's commercial prices to set GSA prices is more complex, subjective, and open to differing interpretations than it looks.

For example, Company EAW manufactures toner cartridges. In August, they had 10,000 cases of toner. The stuff is dated and they needed to get it out of the warehouse, so EAW sold the whole lot at a 25% discount. Two months later, Company A got a 10% discount on 10,000 cases of toner, and a week later Company B got a 10% discount on 6,000 cases of toner. Why? No one remembers for sure.

Which brings me to my final point. Most companies don't really have a handle on what their discounting practices are. Often the reason why a discount was offered is not well documented, nor can the company's discounting practices be described in a clear and definable way.

At least half of the people reading this book will say, "That's us."

The Terms and Conditions Mess

GSA regulations say the contracting officer may consider "terms and conditions" in negotiating fair and reasonable prices. Yet most companies do not have precise, quantifiable terms and conditions for offering discounts.

To complicate matters further, GSA contracting officers are hesitant to base contract pricing on varying terms and conditions because the auditors looking over their shoulders will claim GSA isn't getting the best price for the taxpayer.

Taken together, these factors make price negotiation a messy and painful process. The contracting officer's experience and the experience of the proposal writer and the company's negotiator are important factors in the negotiating process. How well the proposal to GSA articulates discounting practices and terms and conditions related to specific discounts is critical to negotiating prices that are considered fair and reasonable by both parties.

Struggling to Write a GSA Schedule Offer

Beyond the swamp of price and discounting issues, other complexities make GSA proposal writing a struggle.

In some situations, GSA evaluates proposals based on policies that are not published in solicitations. A small business will make a significant investment in writing a proposal and find that it is rejected based on unpublished criteria. When questioned, GSA will say that publishing the criteria is "in the works" or is being reviewed by "legal."

GSA contracting officers and contracting specialists can interpret solicitation provisions and evaluation policies and procedures differently. It is not unheard of for one evaluator to reject a proposal, a second evaluator to ask for additional information, and a third person to accept the same proposal. Some contracting officers may be somewhat flexible in determining fair and reasonable prices, and others may be rigid. Some are experienced and well trained; others will have varying degrees of experience and training.

Your offer must exactly meet all of the requirements laid out in the Schedule solicitation or Request for Proposal. If the RFP calls for 10 copies in 11 pt. Arial font, with Chapter heads in pink, that's exactly what you need to provide. RFPs can often exceed 150 pages, and there can be many quite specific requirements.

The representations and certifications required in a solicitation are often presented in convoluted, bureaucratic language that is difficult to understand.

Sometimes the instructions for preparing and submitting an offer are contained in several sentences, when a clear explanation would require several paragraphs and, in some cases, several pages of text.

Many federal agencies and other organizations—including GSA, the Small Business Administration, and Professional Technical Assistance Centers (PTACs)—try to help small businesses decipher GSA proposal requirements. Such organizations provide assistance to varying degrees, limited by time, resources, and dedicated staff training. The GSA offer process is far too complicated for these types of small business assistance organizations to grasp.

Initiating the Proposal Process

The initial steps in the proposal process are as follows:

1.   Identify which Schedules cover your products or services. As mentioned earlier, this is harder than you might think. Visit www.gsa.gov/schedule and follow the link to Schedules & Other Supplies and Services. Each Schedule has a list of Special Item Numbers (SINs) that are product and service categories related to the Federal Supply Classification System. In effect, the SINs provide a list of the products and service offered under a Schedule.

2.   Review the Federal Supply Schedule for the products and services you want to sell to the feds at GSA Schedules e-Library. Follow the links to FedBizOpps to download the current solicitation document.

3.   Grab a giant cup of coffee and a bottle of aspirin and wade into the pages and pages of red tape and requirements.

4.   Decide whether you want to write the proposal at all, and then decide whether it should be written in-house or outsourced.

Chapter 13

Writing the Proposal

The decision to write a proposal for a Schedule contract is a complex process not to be undertaken lightly. In broad terms, these are the steps you'll have to take:

1.   Gather information on your company's financial condition, product/service prices, sales and discounting practices, and Most Favored customers. (Remember: Contracting officers possess the authority to audit your company's records to check on whatever pricing information you provide.)

2.   Pay a good deal of attention in your proposal to demonstrating why the prices you are proposing to charge the government for your product or service are fair and reasonable in relation to your Most Favored customers. Again, remember that the fundamental goal of the Multiple Award Schedule program is to obtain discount pricing. Therefore, the contracting officer must—and will—analyze the differences between the terms and prices offered to the government and those offered to your company's commercial customers.

3.   Determine what your company's best offer is going to be, and be prepared to negotiate. Define your commercial terms and conditions clearly to justify exceptions to GSA's terms and conditions.

These are the key elements that GSA looks at in the proposal evaluation process. After determining whether your company is basically competent and established, the contracting officer will negotiate with your company, focusing on prices, discounts, warranties, and any other terms unique to your offer.

Pricing is the core of a GSA Schedule contract—both in the original negotiation of prices and in keeping the price the federal government pays in balance with the prices your commercial customers are paying. Change your discounting practices with your Basis of Award commercial customers, and you'll have to do the same for the feds. Understanding this and getting your pricing structure right during the negotiation process can make a significant difference to the bottom line. The rest of the proposal is important, but frequently boils down to check-off-the-box grunt work.

Beginning the Grunt Work

A number of preparatory steps are required before you begin to write a GSA Schedule proposal.

1. Obtain a Data Universal Numbering System (DUNS) Number. The DUNS Number is a unique nine character identification number provided by Dun and Bradstreet. The DUNS website contains information for vendors to obtain DUNS Numbers by telephone or via the Internet (See http://www.dnb.com/US/duns_update/index.html).

2. Register in the Central Contractor Registration (CCR) database and make sure that your CCR registration is up-to-date (See http://www.ccr.gov). In order to register in the CCR, vendors must have a DUNS Number. The CCR collects, validates, stores, and disseminates data in support of agency acquisition missions. Vendors must be registered in the CCR prior to the award of a Schedule contract.

3. Complete the Online Representations and Certifications Application (ORCA) (See https://orca.bpn.gov/login.aspx). ORCA was developed as an Integrated Acquisition Environment (IAE) e-government initiative designed to reduce the administrative burden on vendors and keep them from having to submit the same paper-based representations and certifications repeatedly for various solicitations. Schedule contractors are now required to complete annual representations and certifications electronically via the ORCA website. The representations and certifications must be updated as necessary, but at least annually, to ensure they are kept current, accurate, and complete.

4.   Read the entire Schedule solicitation thoroughly and determine how you are going to respond to each and every requirement. Make sure that all items offered are within the scope of the Schedule solicitation—in other words, don't offer what they haven't asked for.

5.   Contact Open Ratings Inc. for a Past Performance Evaluation. Open Ratings, a Dun and Bradstreet Company, conducts an independent audit of customer references and calculates a rating based upon a statistical analysis of various performance data and survey responses. While some Schedule solicitations contain the form to request an Open Ratings Past Performance Evaluation, vendors may submit an online request directly to Open Ratings.

Multiple Award Schedule Express Program

GSA typically can take anywhere from 45 to 120 days to evaluate a vendor's proposal. Well-prepared and well-documented offers with competitive pricing are more easily evaluated and therefore may be fast-tracked to contract award. Offers requiring lots of corrections and clarifications take longer to be evaluated.

GSA implemented the 30-Day MAS Express Program in early 2007 to speed up the process. As the name implies, the goal of the program is to reduce proposal evaluation time to 30 days. The first phase of the program limited the number of Schedules and types of proposals that could be processed in 30 days. GSA is now in the second phase of the Express Program, with the objective of tripling the scope of the program and allowing for electronic submission of offers.

The MAS Express Program currently only accepts offers for certain Schedules. In order to participate in the MAS Express Program, vendors must meet specific criteria. Vendors must also successfully complete GSA Pathway to Success, an educational seminar designed to assist prospective Schedule contractors in making an informed business decision as to whether obtaining a GSA Schedule contract is in their best interest. Instructions for submitting offers under the MAS Express Program are included in the Schedule solicitations.

Chapter 14

Tracking Your Proposal Submittal

Write down the date your offer was delivered and signed for at GSA and keep this information on hand to track its status. Your offer will be logged in and assigned to a contracting specialist, who reviews the overall offer and notes any deficiencies. This is supposed to occur within two to four weeks of submission, and your company should receive an initial response back within a maximum of 30 days.

However, it almost always takes a gentle reminder to the contracting office responsible for a particular Schedule that an offer was submitted, and how long ago. If there has been no response within 30 days, contact the supervising contracting officer to check the status of your offer. You can ask who has been assigned to your offer, get their contact info, and place a call to this person as well.

GSA will only deal with the person who signed the offer or an authorized negotiator. Nearly every offer submitted will receive a Request for Refinement letter. The letter goes directly to the signatory or the authorized negotiator and outlines the items that need correction or clarification. Go through the letter carefully and identify all of the items that require a response.

Make the corrections and clarifications as soon as possible. Once all revisions to the offer have been made—and this can sometimes take two to three rounds of internal revisions—return the information in the manner requested (fax, mail, email or some combination can be requested).

If GSA accepts your revisions, it's possible that the agency will then sign a contract with you. There's also a chance that some day pigs will fly. Even if you've offered your Most Favored customer prices, GSA will want to enter final negotiations. Remember: GSA always comes back asking for a better price than what you first offered. That doesn't mean you have to give it to them, but the question will be asked, and you might want to leave yourself some wiggle room.

Once negotiations have been successfully concluded, GSA will request that you submit a final revision letter that is signed and dated to finalize the offer.

Winning Just the Beginning

Now here's something that might surprise you after all the work you put into your proposal: Getting a GSA Schedule contract guarantees you nothing. You still have to find those individuals in government who need what you have, establish personal relationships with them, and sell them on your product or solution.

Remember, some of the big volume Schedules have several thousand contractors who will be competing against you. Your Schedule is a valuable tool for closing the sale, but it is not a substitute for making the sale itself. To compete in the federal sales market process, you must:

- Determine who your Schedule competitors are, then identify the similarities, differences, features, warranties, and so on, that distinguish their competing products and services from yours.

- Identify target agencies and make sales calls. Develop relationships with your potential federal customers and determine what they need and want. Convince the customer that you have the solution to their problem, and that a GSA Schedule purchase can be made quickly with a minimum of hassle. Knowing that you have an "already negotiated" contract with GSA and that GSA has determined that your prices are fair and reasonable can frequently put an end-user contemplating a purchase at ease.

- Emphasize price if your company's products are priced low.

If your prices are higher than your competitors, then you need to give the buyer enough ammunition to justify their making a "Best Value" determination. Some examples:

- Fast delivery

- Specific features, warranties

- Quality considerations

- Compatibility with existing products/services

- Trade-in considerations

In short, you need to determine the agency's precise needs and tailor your sales presentation to meet those needs. Low price is the easiest sell if you meet the agency's needs, but you can still make sales with quality and unique features arguments.

Contract Modifications

GSA and the vendor work together to keep a Schedule contract up-to-date through contract modifications. Contract modification requests are submitted to:

- Incorporate changes in GSA terms and conditions (initiated by GSA), usually to the benefit of the vendor

- Add or delete products and services

- Increase or decrease prices (increases are limited by the contract)

- Deal with other proposed legal changes initiated by either party.

Think of a contract modification as a "mini offer." A modification usually requires 5 to10 pages of text versus 150 pages for the original offer, and includes the following essential elements:

- Description of what you want to modify

- Commercial Sales Practice Format for the items being modified

- Commercial price list

- GSA price offer

- Price justification

Contract modifications usually take 30 to 45 days, although they occasionally go through faster. The relative ease of the GSA Schedule contract modification process is one of the big advantages of having a Schedule contract.

Chapter 15

GSA Schedules: Looking Forward

Making purchases through a GSA Schedule contract is increasingly becoming the preferred practice in government purchasing. GSA's recent initiatives and future plans indicate that there is much more growth ahead.

- GSA has implemented a Corporate Schedule that acts effectively as a "Schedule of Schedules" for companies that offer products in many categories.

- GSA Schedules are now "Evergreen" contracts, with a 5-year base and three 5-year option periods. (And why not? If a contractor keeps pricing up-to-date at all times through the contract modification process, why should the contract ever end?)

- Schedule contracts can be used by state and local governments for information technology products and services and for all Schedule products and services required in *emergency conditions*. Most recently, state and local agency use of Schedule 84 Total Solutions for Law Enforcement was authorized.

GSA is fighting a political battle with Congress to expand the Schedule categories that can be used by state and local governments. Give them time; GSA will get it done eventually.

The GSA Industrial Funding Fee paid by vendors is a strong incentive for GSA to grow the Schedule program. GSA uses the IFF war chest to market the Schedule program across the country to federal buyers and vendors. At times the government agency can look like an aggressive commercial company in their sales approach.

Anyone working in the GSA program could give you a laundry list of improvements that would make the program easier for vendors and streamline the proposal evaluation process. The list includes:

- Reduce the number of Schedules from more than 50 to just one. (Don't hold your breath on this one).

- Eliminate the Industrial Funding Fee, and with it GSA's inherent bias toward large businesses. (Another don't-hold-your-breath-while-waiting item.)

- Write solicitations that can be read and understood by someone who doesn't speak and think in bureaucrat-ese.

- As much as possible, automate the proposal evaluation and contract administration process. The lack of a practical digital signature process and the ultraconservative nature of GSA lawyers hinders the complete automation of the proposal submission and evaluation process.

- Gradually eliminate other government-wide multi-vendor contracts. (This would require a re-think on the part of the Office of Management and Budget.)

While it's easy to identify ways to improve GSA Schedule implementation, it's extremely difficult to move toward any kind of change. GSA is working hard to improve the program. GSA program managers know what to do to streamline the program but are hampered by entrenched bureaucratic responses and legal precedents. Any changes in their approach to terms and conditions would have to be reflected in more than 18,000 existing contracts..

Providing a set of short concise instructions in eOffer or as introductory content in solicitation documents would help vendors understand what GSA needs and why. In addition, it would help if GSA developed a standard set of vendor instructions in plain English in a single section of Schedule solicitations.

The Abu Ghraib Iraq prisoner interrogation and abuse scandal shook GSA to the core. Congress and federal auditors immediately piled on when the story broke. As a result, GSA contracting officers have become quite audit shy. This, in turn, caused an undue number of "scope of work" proposal rejections and demands for *Most Favorable Customer* pricing that seemed unreasonable to vendors.

The federal procurement program is understaffed and creaking at the seams. However, Congress and the Executive Branch know how important the program is to the government. If you're a small- to medium-sized business, you can expect good things to come from the GSA Schedule program. Despite the problems, GSA Schedule contracting is a groundbreaking element of the federal procurement program.

Program improvements will evolve slowly, but GSA knows what is needed and the resistance to change appears to be diminishing. The audit-shy syndrome may gradually fade with time as the bureaucracy slowly forgets the scope of work Abu Ghraib scandal

Small Biz and the GSA

Why not encourage and support small business participation in GSA Schedule contracting by loosening the experience and number-of-years-in-business requirements somewhat? Why not have 100,000 GSA Schedule holders rather than fewer than 20,000? Why not fund and train the over 200 Procurement Technical Assistance Centers (PTACs) across the country to assist small businesses in obtaining a GSA Schedule?

GSA is conflicted about encouraging small businesses. Increased participation of small businesses would increase Industrial Funding Fees, but not by much, and not in direct proportion to the increase in Schedule holders—and thus paperwork. The current, mostly paper-based Schedule submission/evaluation/negotiation processing system can barely handle the number of offers now.

"We have lost your paperwork; would you please resubmit your offer?" is not an uncommon communication to vendors who have submitted an offer. GSA lawyers still prefer paper over electronic submissions, and are a drag on significant automation improvements.

One answer to this dilemma is to eliminate the Industrial Funding Fee as the funding method for the GSA Schedule Program. Dramatic, yes. But money could be funneled from the notoriously ineffective Small Business Administration to fund the GSA Schedule Program and PTACs. The government's so-called small business "advocates" at SBA typically see their mission as helping small business in general, not individual small businesses, and thus offer very little assistance to vendors looking to break into the federal market.

Eliminating IFF funding would also eliminate the inherent bias GSA has for large businesses that produce a lot of IFF dollars.

Revamping the Schedule system so that it is not required to pay its own way is not a new idea. Unfortunately it is such a good idea that actually moving it to fruition may be a dream. It would take Congressional action, and Congress usually does the expedient or politically popular thing rather than the right thing.

Fedmarket.com Services

Fedmarket.com offers a range of services to companies seeking GSA Schedule contracts.

GSA Proposal Preparation eLab

Fedmarket.com helps companies fulfill the requirements and complete the paperwork necessary to be awarded a GSA Schedule contract. Once you register for our three-day workshop, we provide a detailed Request for Information (RFI) that enables you to fully prepare for the workshop prior to your arrival. The RFI outlines the required corporate data, pricing information, and staffing information that provide the core of a winning GSA proposal.

Once you arrive at our teaching lab, each participant is assigned a computer. During the three-day course of instruction and hands-on assistance from our GSA-expert staff, eLab participants are able to write winning proposals and learn crucial negotiating tactics.

With our guidance, attendees are able to complete their GSA offer during the three-day workshop. If you are a procrastinator, the GSA eLab is the solution for you. Fedmarket.com's GSA proposal Preparation eLab is offered each month at the Federal Sales Academy in Bethesda, Maryland, and quarterly in Las Vegas, Nevada.

More than 1,000 companies have sent people to attend Fedmarket.com's GSA Schedule eLab. Here's why:

1. One problem our eLab attendees regularly present us with is that writing a proposal to GSA is the kind of task that is constantly postponed, over and over, often for years. It's an easy thing to do, because there is no deadline; a GSA proposal can be submitted at any

time. Therefore postponing proposal writing to another day is always convenient. A refrain we often here is: "We begin proposal writing late in the day, because day-to-day responsibilities always take precedence. When we begin dealing with the red tape, the confusing solicitation requirements, and the details of writing a technical approach, postponement to another day becomes inevitable and a huge relief.

2.   FedMarket's eLab provides the opportunity for your designated proposal writing staff person to devote his or her entire time and energy to writing a compelling proposal in a supportive, guided environment.

3.   FedMarket.com's eLab is an extremely cost-effective approach to breaking into the federal marketplace and is less expensive than alternative approaches to obtaining a GSA schedule.

4.   Participants in Fedmarket.com's eLabs learn the nuances of GSA schedule proposal preparation, negotiation, contract administration, and GSA contract compliance. The eLab helps participants write winning proposals to GSA and to successfully manage contracts after award.

 Call a Fedmarket representative at (888) 661-4094, ext. 8, for specific dates and more information about the three-day workshop.

GSA Wizard™

Our GSA Wizard™ is a proprietary software product that assists individuals and companies in preparing GSA Schedule proposals. The product was designed specifically for companies that decide to prepare their GSA Schedule offer on their own in an effort to save costs. The Wizard enables companies that don't have a working knowledge of the GSA Schedule process to prepare an offer. Our software systematically walks the customer through GSA's solicitation and, through detailed instructions, templates, and illustrated examples, assists the customer in responding to the requests for information found in the GSA solicitation. The cost of the software includes five hours of consulting time, via telephone or email, with our GSA specialists.

Full-Service GSA Proposal Preparation

Fedmarket.com offers full-service consulting to companies that would prefer to let our experts tackle the GSA Schedule offer. Our specialists take the lead in preparing your corporate offer. We handle the entire process--from proposal preparation to, perhaps most importantly, the challenging contract negotiations with GSA. We work with your staff and GSA's contracting officer from start to finish.

GSA Electronic Proposal Preparation Assistance

Fedmarket.com's "Preparation Assistance" option is a cost-sensitive alternative to our full-service GSA consulting services. We prepare the Schedule offer for you using corporate data and information you provide us. We return an electronic copy of the completed proposal for you to submit and negotiate on your own.

GSA Consulting Services

Fedmarket.com offers consulting services at an hourly rate or fixed price basis to assist companies in solving GSA Schedule related problems. Consulting services include proposal refinement, proposal evaluation, price negotiation, contract compliance policy and procedure development, contract administration, and audit preparation.

FedBuyingIntelligence Online: Who Buys What You Sell?

FedBuyingIntelligence (FBI) is a subscription service that brings focus and precision to your sales efforts.

FBI quickly identifies the federal buyers who buy what you sell—and tells you how often they make those purchases. For each of your company's federal supply codes, FBI provides a complete purchasing history, rich with critical information such as buyer contact names, phone numbers, email addresses, agency names and geographic locations. Browse this information online, or download it for use in your contact database or other contact applications.

Assembling intelligence data on your own takes an enormous amount of time and effort. FBI streamlines this difficult process by giving you access to current data that will provide you with the tools to succeed in the federal marketplace.

FedBuyingIntelligence (FBI) is the most powerful sales tool in the federal market. It searches five years of public bid data and tells you who bought what. Enter your product or service using keywords, Product/Service Codes, or NAICS Codes, and find the solicitations and awards for the contracting officers and Contract Specialists who bought your product/service. Contact data including telephone number and email address is provided for each buyer in a downloadable spreadsheet.

FBI tells you:

- Which federal buyers have purchased your products or services.

- What they purchased.

- When they purchased it.

- How much they paid.

- Which agency the buyers work for.

- How to contact the buyers.

FBI government buyer information includes:

- First and last name

- Address

- Phone and fax

- Email

- Office and agency information

- Recent contract awards

Call us at toll free at (888) 661-4094 x 8 for more information or visit http://www.fedmarket.com/products/gsa_index.shtml.

Appendix A

GSA Management Service Centers

Center	Schedule Responsibilities	Contact
Information Technology (IT) Acquisition Center	Schedule 70 General Purpose Commercial Information Technology Equipment, Software, and Services Solicitation Number: FCIS-JB-980001-B	CENTER FOR IT SCHEDULE PROGRAM ATTN.: BOOCO Crystal Plaza #4, Room 606 2220 Crystal Drive Arlington, VA 22202 (703) 605-2700 it.center@gsa.gov
Management Services Center	Schedule 874 Mission Oriented Business Integrated Services (MOBIS) Solicitation Number: TFTP-MC-000874-B	Organizational Services Division, 10FTB 400 15TH SW Auburn, WA 98001-6599 (800) 241-7246 Fax: (253) 931-7111
	Schedule 871 Professional Engineering Services (PES) Solicitation Number: FCXB-B2-990001-B	Bid Custodian (10FT-BID) 400 15th Street SW Auburn, WA 98001-6599 (800) 241-7246 pes@gsa.gov
	Schedule 738 II Language Services Solicitation Number: TFTP-GC-07382-B	400 15th Street SW Auburn, WA 98001-6599 (800) 241-7246 language@gsa.gov
	Schedule 899 Environmental Services Solicitation Number: TFTP-EW-990899-B	Environmental Services Branch 400 15th Street SW Auburn, WA 98001-6599 (800) 241-7246 environmental@gsa.gov

Center	Schedule Responsibilities	Contact
	Schedule 874 V Logistics Worldwide (LOGWORLD) Solicitation Number: TFTP-MB-008745-B	Logistics Worldwide Branch 400 15th Street SW Auburn, WA 98001-6599 (800) 241-7246 logworld@gsa.gov
	Schedule 00CORP Consolidated Schedule Solicitation Number: FCO-00-CORP-0000C	400 15th Street SW Auburn, WA 98001-6599 (800) 241-7246 consolidated@gsa.gov
	Schedule 871 II Energy Services Solicitation Number: TFTD-EJ-00871-B	400 15th Street SW Auburn, WA 98001-6599 (800) 241-7246 energy@gsa.gov
Services Acquisition Center	Schedule 520 Financial and Business Solutions (FABS) Solicitation Number: FCXB-F4-020002-B	Center for Services Acquisition (QSAB) 2200 Crystal Drive, Suite 706 Arlington, VA 22202 (703) 605-9500 fabs@gsa.gov
Greater Southwest Acquisition Center	Schedule 56 Buildings and Building Materials/Industrial Services and Supplies Solicitation Number: 7FCI-03-0056-B	Building Materials and Hospitality Division: (7FCC) 819 Taylor Street, Room 7A37 Fort Worth, TX 76102-6114 JoAnne Offill (817) 574-2482 joanne.offill@gsa.gov
	Schedule 73 Food Service, Hospitality, Cleaning Equipment and Supplies, Chemicals, and Services Solicitation Number: 7FCM-C4-03-0073-B	Building Materials and Hospitality Division: (7FCC) 819 Taylor Street, Room 7A37 Fort Worth, TX 76102-6114 JoAnne Offill (817) 574-2482 joanne.offill@gsa.gov
	Schedule 084 Total Solutions for Law Enforcement, Security, Facility Management Systems, Fire, Rescue, Special Purpose Clothing, Marine Craft and	7QSAB-T4 819 Taylor Street, Room 7A37 Fort Worth, TX 76102-6114 Teresa Hill teresa.hill@gsa.gov

Center	Schedule Responsibilities	Contact
	Emergency/ Disaster Response Solicitation Number: 7FCI-L3-03-0084-B	(817) 574-2451
	Schedule 541 Advertising & Integrated Marketing Solutions (AIMS) Solicitation Number: FCXA-M2-030001-B	7QSAC-B7 819 Taylor Street, Room 7A37 Fort Worth, TX 76102-6114 JoAnn Stanley (817) 574-2336 joann.stanley@gsa.gov
	Schedule 736 Temporary Administrative and Professional Staffing Services (TAPS) Solicitation Number: 7FCM-N6-03-0736-B	7QSAC 819 Taylor Street, Room 7A37 Fort Worth, TX 76102-6114 Frank Wilson(7QSAC-F5) Phone: (817) 574-2388 FAX: (817)574-2342 Email: Frank.Wilson@gsa.gov
	Schedule 66 Scientific Equipment and Services Solicitation Number: FCB-C4-070066-B	819 Taylor Street, Room 7A37 Fort Worth, TX 76102-6114 JoAnn Stanley (817) 574-2336 joann.stanley@gsa.gov
Center for Facilities Maintenance and Hardware	Schedule 51V Hardware SuperStore Solicitation Number: 6FEC-E6-060173-B	6QSA-H1 1500 E. Bannister Road, Room SBE16-1 Kansas City, MO 64131 Ellen Upchurch (816) 926-7808 ellie.upchurch@gsa.gov
	Schedule 03FAC Facilities Maintenance and Management Solicitation Number: 6FEC-E6-030292-B	1500 E. Bannister Road, Kansas City, MO 64131 Jay Willingham (816) 823-1285 jay.willingham@gsa.gov
National Furniture Center	Schedule 58 I Professional Audio/Video, Telecommunications, and Security Solutions Solicitation Number:	3FNG 20 N. 8TH ST. Philadelphia, PA 19107 Robert Gever (215) 446-5206

Center	Schedule Responsibilities	Contact
	3FNGRG020001B	robert.gever@gsa.gov
	Schedule 71 I Office Furniture Solicitation Number: 3FNG-RG-020001-B	1901 South Bell Street, Suite 403 Arlington, VA 22202 Glenda Lambert 703-605-9236 glenda.lambert@gsa.gov
	Schedule 71 II Household and Quarters Furniture Solicitation Number: 3FNH-F6-02002-B	3FNH-CO 2200 Crystal Drive, Ste.400, Crystal Plaza #4, Arlington, VA 22202 Thomas Murray (703) 605-9247 e-mail thomas.murray@gsa.gov
	Schedule 71 II H Packaged Furniture Solicitation Number: 3FNH-A3-00001-B	3FNHA-CO 1901 S. Bell Street, Suite 403 Arlington, VA 20406-0003 Helen Zivkoviche 703-605-9293 Helen.Zivkoviche@gsa.gov
	Schedule 71 II K Comprehensive Furniture Management Services Solicitation Number: 3FNC-B3-003001-B	2200 Crystal Drive, Suite 400 Arlington, VA 22202 Linda Valdes (703) 605-9278 Linda.valdes@gsa.gov
	Schedule 71 III Special Use Furniture—Library, Hospital, Mailroom, Preschool and Classroom, Cafeteria, and Industrial Solicitation Number: 3FNG-F6-010003-B	3FNHD-CO 1901 S. Bell Street, Suite 403, Arlington, VA 20406-0003 Walter Young 703-605-9292 walter.young@gsa.gov
	Schedule 71 III E Miscellaneous Furniture—Security Filing Cabinets, Safes, Vault Doors, Map and Plan Files and Accessories, COMSEC Containers, and Special Access Control Containers Solicitation Number: 3FNG-BA-030001-B	3QSAB Household & Industrial Furniture Procurement Division 2200 Crystal Drive, Ste. 400 Arlington, VA 22202 Sabrina Williams 703-605-9287 sabrina.william@gsa.gov
	Schedule 72 I A Floor Coverings—Carpets, Rugs,	3FNHF 2200 Crystal Drive, Suite 400

Center	Schedule Responsibilities	Contact
	Carpet Tiles and Carpet Cushions, Vinyl and Rubber Tiles and Rolls, Mats and Matting (with and without logos) Solicitation Number: 3FNH-F3-00F002-B	Arlington, VA 22202 Susan Anderson Susan.Anderson@gsa.gov
	Schedule 72 II Furnishings—Window Treatments, Wall Art, Artificial Plants, Lamps Solicitation Number: 3FNG-PL-990008-B	3QSAB 2200 Crystal Drive, Suite 400 Arlington, Virginia 22202 Darlene Walsh 703-605-9281 darlene.walsh@gsa.gov
	Schedule 36 The Office, Imaging and Document Solutions—Office Equipment Products and Services, and Document Management Products and Services Solicitation Number: 3FNJ-C1-00-0001-B	3QSAC The Strawbridge Bldg. 20 N. 8th Street, Room 1029 Philadelphia, PA 19107-3191 Shannon Stanford Phone: (215) 446-5058 Fax: (215) 446-5112 shannon.stanford@gsa.gov
	Schedule 78 Sports, Promotional, Outdoor, Recreational, Trophies, and Signs (SPORTS) Solicitation Number: 7FCM-M5-03-0078-B	3FNG The Strawbridge Bldg. 20 N. 8th Street, Room 1029 Philadelphia, PA 19107-3191 Monica Gormley Phone 215-446-5087 FAX: 215-829-2787 monica.gormley@gsa.gov
Office Supplies and Administrative Services Center	Schedule 69 Training Aids and Devices; Instructor-Led Training; Course Development; Test Administration Solicitation Number: 2FYA-06-000069-B-R2	2QSAA 26 Federal Plaza, Room 19-100 New York, NY 10278 Tony Zaza 212.264.3548 tony.zaza@gsa.gov
	Schedule 738 X Human Resources and EEO Services Solicitation Number:	26 Federal Plaza, Room 19-100 New York, NY 10278 Henry Pierre-Louis, Section Chief 212-264-2670

Center	Schedule Responsibilities	Contact
	2FYA-WA-0600738X-B	
	Schedule 75 Office Products/Supplies and Services and New Products/Technology (Includes Restroom Products) Solicitation Number: 2FYB-BU-05-0001-B	Office Products Acquisition Branch (2QSAB) 26 Federal Plaza, Room 19-128 New York, N.Y. 10278 Marino Abreu 212-264-3026 marino.abreu@gsa.gov
	Schedule 67 Photographic Equipment— Cameras, Photographic Printers and Related Supplies and Services (Digital and Film-Based) Solicitation Number: 2FYB-BJ-03-0001-B	Office Products Acquisition Branch (2QSAB) 26 Federal Plaza, Room 19-128 New York, N.Y. 10278 Margo Michelsen-Clare 212-264-8732 margo.michelsen-clare@gsa.gov
	Schedule 76 Publication Media Solicitation Number: 2FYA-JD-060001-B	26 Federal Plaza, Room 19-100 New York, NY 10278 Peter Mare 212.264.2689 E-mail peter.mare@gsa.gov
	Schedule 81 I B Shipping, Packaging and Packing Supplies—Bags, Sacks, Cartons, Crates, Packaging and Packing Bulk Material Solicitation Number: 2FYB-DJ-05-0008-B	Office Products Acquisition Branch (2QSAB) 26 Federal Plaza, Room 19-128 New York, N.Y. 10278 Ruth Albert 212-264-3515 ruth.albert@gsa.gov
GSA Automotive	Schedule 23V Vehicular Multiple Award Schedule Solicitation Number: FFAH-C2-99-0235-B	FFAH 1901 S. Bell Street, Room 600 Arlington, VA 22202 Ira Herman (703) 605-2986 ira.herman@gsa.gov
	Schedule 26 I Pneumatic Tires: New for Passenger Vehicles; New and Retread for Light Trucks, Medium Trucks, and Buses Solicitation Number: FCAP-S2-96-2601	FFAH 2200 Crystal Drive, Suite 1006 Arlington, VA 22202 Cheryl Harris (703) 605-2984 cheryl.harris@gsa.gov

Center	Schedule Responsibilities	Contact
	Schedule 751 Leasing of Automobiles and Light Trucks Solicitation Number: FFAP-W1-00768-N	Office of Acquisition Operations 2200 Crystal Drive, Suite 1006 Arlington, VA 22202 Laurel Weiskopf 703-605-5721 Laurel.Weiskopf@gsa.gov
Office of Transportation and Property Management	Schedule 48 Transportation, Delivery and Relocation Solutions (TDRS) Solicitation Number: FBGT-GG-050001-B	Transportation Acquisition Branch (FBGT) 2200 Crystal Drive, Crystal Plaza 4, Room 300 Arlington, VA 20406 703.605-5616 Lisa Romano (703) 605-2920 lisa.romano@gsa.gov
	Schedule 599 Travel Services Solutions Solicitation Number: FBGT-RK-040001-B	Office of Transportation & Property Management Contracting Division (FBG) 1941 Jefferson Davis Highway, Room 812 Arlington, VA 22202 Brenda Samuels (703) 605-2918 brenda.samuels@gsa.gov
VA FSS	Schedule 621 I Professional and Allied Healthcare Staffing Services Solicitation Number: 797-FSS-00-0115-R2	VA FSS 621 I Help Desk (708) 786-7722
	Schedule 65 I B Pharmaceuticals and Drugs Solicitation Number: M5-Q50A-03-R1	Robert Setterfield (703) 786-4955 Robert.setterfiled@gsa.gov
	65 II A Solicitation Medical Equipment and Supplier Schedule Number: 797-FSS-99-0025-R4	Department of Veterans Affairs National Acquisition Center (049A2-2) P.O. Box 76, Building 37 Hines, IL 60141 Paul Skalman (708) 786-5247 paul.skalman@gsa.gov

Center	Schedule Responsibilities	Contact
	Schedule 65 II C Dental Equipment and Supplier Solicitation Number: 797-652C-04-0001	Department of Veterans Affairs National Acquisition Center (049A2-2) P.O. Box 76, Building 37 Hines, IL 60141 Phone: Federal Supply Schedule Helpdesk (708) 786-7737 Helpdesk.ammhinfss@va.gov
	Schedule 65 II F Patient Mobility Devices -- (Including Medical and Dental X-Ray Film) Solicitation Number: 797-652F-05-0001-R1	Department of Veterans Affairs National Acquisition Center (049A1F1) P.O. Box 76, Building 37 Hines, IL 60141 Sandra Perkins (708) 786-4958 Sandra.Perkins@gsa.gov
	Schedule 65 V A X-Ray Equipment and Supplies - - (Including Medical and Dental X-Ray Film) Solicitation Number: 797-655A-03-0001	Department of Veterans Affairs National Acquisition Center (049A1F1) P.O. Box 76, Building 37 Hines, IL 60141 Sandra Perkins (708) 786-4958 Sandra.Perkins@gsa.gov
	Schedule 65 VII S Testing and Measurement Equipment, Aviation Instruments and Equipment Aircraft Components, Maintenance and Repair Services, and Unmanned Scientific Vehicles Solicitation Number: M5-Q52A-04-R1	Department of Veterans Affairs National Acquisition Center (049A1F1) P.O. Box 76 Hines, IL 60141 W. R. (Bob) Satterfield, III (708) 786-4955 bob.satterfield@med.va.gov

Appendix B

Vendor Sales by GSA Schedule

Schedule Number	Description	Value of Sales in FY 2007
00CORP	The Consolidated Schedule	$869,599,165
03FAC	Facilities Maintenance and Management	$151,716,262
23 V	Vehicular Multiple Award Schedule (VMAS)	$125,765,128
26 I	Tires, Pneumatic (New), For Passenger, Light Truck, Medium Truck, and Bus, and Retread Services	$13,115,504
36	The Office, Imaging and Document Solution	$910,582,194
48	Transportation, Delivery and Relocation Solutions	$648,033,408
51 V	Hardware Superstore	$626,643,979
520	Financial and Business Solutions (FABS)	$961,669,496
541	Advertising and Integrated Marketing Solutions (AIMS)	$520,040,266
56	Buildings and Building Materials/Industrial Services and Supplies	$453,413,673
58 I	Professional Audio/Video, Telecommunications, and security Solutions	$183,382,678
599	Travel Solutions	$272,669,168
66	Scientific Equipment and Services	$693,596,649
66 II J	Test and Measurement Equipment, Aviation Instruments and Equipment Aircraft Components, Maintenance and Repair Services, and Unmanned	$166,526

Schedule Number	Description	Value of Sales in FY 2007
	Scientific Vehicles	
66 II N	Chemistry, Biochemistry, Clinical Instruments, General Purpose Laboratory Instruments, Laboratory Furnishings and Accessories, and Related Services	$6,992,461
66 II Q	Geophysical, Environmental Analysis Equipment and Services – Geophysical Environmental, Analysis and Hazard Equipment	$0
67	Photographic Equipment – Cameras, Photographic Printers and Related Supplies and Services (Digital and Film-Based)	$47,123,423
69	Training Aids and Devices, Instructor-Led Training; Course Development; Test Administration – Programmed learning devices	$227,450,362
70	General Purpose Commercial Information Technology Equipment, Software, and Services – Pursuant to Section 211 of the e-Gov Act of 2002, Cooperative Purchasing provides authorized State and local government entities access to information technology items offered through GSA's Schedule 70 and the Corporate contracts for associated special item numbers.	$16,401,176,473
71 I	Office Furniture	$891,348,170
71 II	Household and Quarters Furniture	$96,162,034
71 II H	Packaged Furniture	$91,107,974
71 II K	Comprehensive Furniture Management Services (CFMS)	$35,213,866
71 III	Special Use Furniture	$120,673,393
71 III E	Miscellaneous Furniture	$27,689,533
72 I A	Floor Coverings – Carpet Rugs, Carpet Tiles and Carpet Cushions	$47,880,463
72 II	Furnishings	20,099,909
73	Food Service, Hospitality, Cleaning Equipment and Supplies, Chemicals and Services – Food Service	$202,877,519

Schedule Number	Description	Value of Sales in FY 2007
	Equipment, Supplies, and Services	
736	Temporary Administrative And Professional Staffing (TAPS) – Temporary Administrative and Professional Staffing Services	$117,262,259
738 II	Language Services	$144,677,093
738 X	Human Resources and Equal Employment Opportunity Services	$177,408,265
75	Office Products/Supplies and Services and New Products/Technology – Schedule 75 now includes Videotapes, Audiotapes, tape Cartridges, Diskettes/Optical Disks, Disk Packs, Disk Cartridges, Anti-Glare Screens, cleaning Equipment and Supplies, Ergonomic Devices, Next Day Desktop Delivery of Office Supplies, and Restroom Products such as Roll Toilet Tissue Dispensers, Toilet Tissue, Paper Towels, Toilet Seat Covers, Facial tissues, and Soaps for Restroom Dispensers	$574,126,993
751	Leasing of Automobiles and Light Trucks	$7,668,410
76	Publication Media	$118,175,376
78	Sports, Promotional, Outdoor, Recreation, Trophies, and Signs (SPORTS) – Trophies, Awards, Presentations, Promotional Products, Briefcases and Carrying Cases, Trade Show Displays and Exhibit Systems And all Related Products	$307,229,020
81 I B	Shipping, Packaging and Packing Supplies – Bags, Sacks, Cartons, Crates, Packaging And Packing Bulk Material	$95,026,106
84	Total Solutions for Law Enforcement, Security, Facilities, Management, Fire, Rescue, Clothing, Marine Craft and Emergency/Disaster Response – Marine Craft and Equipment	$2,233,953,472
871	Professional Engineering Services	$2,716,063,410
871 II	Energy Services	$0
873	Laboratory Testing and Analysis Services	$10,316,804

Schedule Number	Description	Value of Sales in FY 2007
874	Mission Oriented Business Integrated Services (MOBIS)	3,606,048,871
874 V	Logistics Worldwide (LOGWORLD)	$647,097,520
899	Environmental Services	$339,983,517

Appendix C

GSA Solicitation (RFP) Requirements

Schedule	Solicitation (RFP) Requirements
00 Consolidated Schedule	• Must propose or have 2 or more schedules business lines to participate in the Consolidated Schedule program • Requirements that fall within the scope of more than one schedule for acquiring a total solution. Contractors under this schedule hold a single contract that includes two or more combined services from schedules such as: Facilities Maintenance, Office Imaging and Document Solutions, Training, Information Technology, Publications, Financial and Business Solutions, Advertising and Integrated Marketing Solutions, Language, Human Resources, Professional Engineering, MOBIS, Logworld, and Environmental. • All items under Schedule 23 V are excluded from the consolidated solicitation. • See individual schedule requirements below for specifics (e.g. MOBIS, IT70)
03 Facilities Maintenance and Management	• 10-20 Invoices minimum requirement • 3 years of audited financial statements (if available) – like to review balance sheet and income statements– like to review balance sheet and income statements • a minimum of two (2) years of relevant experience • Key personnel/individual experience may be substituted for corporate experience. • 2 project descriptions for each SIN offered. The projects must have been completed within the past two years or can be ongoing projects. For ongoing projects under a contract with a base year and option years, the base year must have been completed. For multi-year contracts or task orders, the first year must have been

Schedule	Solicitation (RFP) Requirements
	completed.
	• If seeking to offer SIN 811-002 you must submit an offer, which includes at least 3 of the specific tasks as listed in this SIN. Must also manage a facility for a continuous period of one year or more for a period of 8 hours a day or more.
36 Office, Imaging and Document Solutions	• 3 years of audited financial statements (if available) • a minimum of two (2) years of relevant experience • Key personnel/individual experience may be substituted for corporate experience. • 2 project descriptions for each SIN offered. The projects must have been completed within the past two years or can be ongoing projects. For ongoing projects under a contract with a base year and option years, the base year must have been completed. For multi-year contracts or task orders, the first year must have been completed.
48 Transportation, Delivery and Relocation Solutions (TDRS)	• 3 years of financial statements • Personal experience of staff is accepted for the services being offered. • 3 Project descriptions each must be a value of $25k. 2 of 3 descriptions must have been completed within the past two years.
520 FABS	• 3 years of audited financial statements (if available) • a minimum of two (2) years of relevant experience • Key personnel/individual experience may be substituted for corporate experience. • SIN 520-6 Professional Legal Services – Your firm must be a licensed law firm. • SIN 520-7 Financial and Performance Audits – Your firm must be a licensed CPA firm • 2 project descriptions for each SIN offered. The projects must have been completed within the past two years or can be ongoing projects. For ongoing projects under a contract with a base year and option years, the base year must have been completed. For multi-year contracts or task orders, the first year must have been completed.
541 AIMS	• 3 years of audited financial statements (if available)

Schedule	Solicitation (RFP) Requirements
	• a minimum of two (2) years of relevant experience • 2 project descriptions for each SIN offered. The projects must have been completed within the past two years or can be ongoing projects. For ongoing projects under a contract with a base year and option years, the base year must have been completed. For multi-year contracts or task orders, the first year must have been completed.
599 Travel	• 3 years of financial statements • 3 Project descriptions each must be a value of $25k. • 2 of 3 descriptions must have been completed within the past two years. • Personal experience of staff is accepted for the services being offered.
621 I Professional and Allied Healthcare Staffing Services	• You must have professional malpractice insurance with minimum coverage of $1 million per occurrence and $3 million in the aggregate. • Your corporation must also have automobile liability insurance with coverage of at least $200,000 per person (employee) and $500,000 per occurrence for bodily injury and $20,000 per occurrence for property damage • You must have one year of corporate experience, at a minimum. • You must be capable of providing your services in at least one entire state. • You must provide a minimum of three references for your most recently-performed contract (or engagement). The contract must have been performed within the past two years
65 II A Medical Equipment and Supplies	• Small Business Set-Aside for SINs: A-13a, A-13c, A-37, A-38, A-43, A-63, A-75, A-78 and A-82 – You may not offer these SINs if it is determined your firm is a large business.
66: SCIENTIFIC EQUIPMENT AND SERVICES	• 873: you are now required to have at least $25,000 in previous sales for the same or similar work. • 873: 3 years of corporate experience in delivering laboratory testing and related services • 873: Personal experience of staff is accepted. • Covers: Test and Measurement Equipment, Unmanned Scientific Vehicles; Laboratory Instruments, Furnishings and LIMS;

Schedule	Solicitation (RFP) Requirements
	Geophysical and Environmental Analysis Equipment; and Mechanical, Chemical, Electrical, and Geophysical Testing Services
69 Training	• 3 years of audited financial statements (if available) • a minimum of two (2) years of relevant experience • Key personnel/individual experience may be substituted for corporate experience. • 2 project descriptions for each SIN offered. The projects must have been completed within the past two years or can be ongoing projects. For ongoing projects under a contract with a base year and option years, the base year must have been completed. For multi-year contracts or task orders, the first year must have been completed.
IT70	• 3 years of audited financial statements (if available) • a minimum of two (2) years of relevant experience • 2 project descriptions for each SIN offered. The projects must have been completed within the past two years or can be ongoing projects. For ongoing projects under a contract with a base year and option years, the base year must have been completed. For multi-year contracts or task orders, the first year must have been completed.
71 II K Comprehensive Furniture Management Services	• Products may only be offered with Services under SIN 712-5. • PRODUCTS OFFERED MUST BE CURRENTLY be ON-SCHEDULE UNDER GSA SCHEDULE CONTRACTS 36, 58-I, 71-I, 71-II, 71-III, 71-III-E, 72-I-A, or 72-II. • Firm's most recent Income Statement and Balance Sheet or Annual Report
75 Office Supplies	• 1 year of audited financial statements (if available) • Provide three (3) high volume invoices for the previous three (3) months from the company's most favored customers(s) identified in the offer, prior to proposal submittal, for the products you are offering which demonstrates high sales potentials.
736 TAPS	• 3 years in business and services being offered • This Solicitation is 100% Set-Aside for Small Business • employer liability , General Liability , include copies of Certificate of Insurance

Schedule	Solicitation (RFP) Requirements
	• Current copies of proof of coverage for Workers Compensation for each state where you are offering locations.
738 II Language Services	• 3 years of audited financial statements (if available)
	• a minimum of two (2) years of relevant experience
	• 2 project descriptions for each SIN offered. The projects must have been completed within the past two years or can be ongoing projects. For ongoing projects under a contract with a base year and option years, the base year must have been completed. For multi-year contracts or task orders, the first year must have been completed. Key personnel/individual experience may be substituted for corporate experience.
738X Human Resources and EEO Services	• 3 years of audited financial statements (if available)
	• a minimum of two (2) years of relevant experience
	• Key personnel/individual experience may be substituted for corporate experience.
	• 2 project descriptions for each SIN offered. The projects must have been completed within the past two years or can be ongoing projects. For ongoing projects under a contract with a base year and option years, the base year must have been completed. For multi-year contracts or task orders, the first year must have been completed.
81 IB Shipping, Packaging and Packing Supplies—Bags, Sacks, Cartons, Crates, Packaging and Packing Bulk Material	• **Only if offering: SIN 617 10 - PACKAGING SERVICES and/or SIN 617 13 - unique IDENTIFICATION (uid)/RADIO FREQUENCY IDENTIFICATION (RFID)**
	• 3 Project descriptions, all must have been completed within the past two years.
	•
84 Total Law Enforcement	• SINs (guard services) 246-52 and 246-54
	• Your firm must have a minimum of three (3) years of corporate experience if offering Guard Services.
871 Professional Engineering Services	• 3 years of audited financial statements (if available)
	• a minimum of two (2) years of relevant experience
	• Key personnel/individual experience may be substituted for corporate experience.

Schedule	Solicitation (RFP) Requirements
	• 2 project descriptions for each SIN offered. The projects must have been completed within the past two years or can be ongoing projects. For ongoing projects under a contract with a base year and option years, the base year must have been completed. For multi-year contracts or task orders, the first year must have been completed.
871 II Energy	• Last Year financial statements or audited report • 3 Project descriptions, 2 of 3 descriptions must have been completed within the past two years.
874 MOBIS	• 3 years of audited financial statements (if available) • A minimum of 3 years of experience in providing MOBIS professional services to either a government or commercial entity • 2 project descriptions for each SIN offered. The projects must have been completed within the past two years or can be ongoing projects. For ongoing projects under a contract with a base year and option years, the base year must have been completed. For multi-year contracts or task orders, the first year must have been completed.
874V Logistics	• 2-3 years of audited financial statements • 2 Project descriptions, each description must have been completed within the past 5 years.
899 Environmental Services	• 3 years of audited financial statements (if available) • a minimum of two (2) years of relevant experience • 2 project descriptions for each SIN offered. The projects must have been completed within the past two years or can be ongoing projects. For ongoing projects under a contract with a base year and option years, the base year must have been completed. For multi-year contracts or task orders, the first year must have been completed.

Appendix D

Organizations Eligible to Use GSA Sources of Supply and Services

1. <u>Purpose</u>. This Order provides definitions and listings of agencies and other activities authorized
to use GSA sources of supply and services. It also provides definitive guidelines concerning eligibility requirements.

2. <u>Cancellation</u>. ADM 4800.2D is canceled.

3. <u>Background</u>. Section 201 of the Federal Property and Administrative Services Act of 1949, as amended (the Property Act) authorizes the Administrator of General Services (Administrator) to procure and supply personal property and non-personal services for executive agencies and other Federal agencies, mixed-ownership Government corporations as identified in the Government Corporation Control Act, the District of Columbia, and qualified nonprofit agencies for the blind or other severely handicapped for use in making or providing an approved commodity or service to the Government. Other organizations may be eligible pursuant to other sections of the Property Act or by reason of enabling statutory authority.

4. <u>Nature of revision</u>. These revisions update the listings of organizations determined eligible to use GSA sources of supply and services.

5. Definition. GSA sources of supply and services are defined as those support programs administered by GSA and prescribed in the Federal Property Management Regulations (FPMR), 41 CFR Parts 101-26--Procurement Sources and Programs, 101-35--Telecommunications, 101-39--Interagency Fleet Management Systems (GSA Fleet),101-40--Transportation and Traffic Management, 101-42 through 101-46, 101-48,

and 101-49, Utilization and Disposal Programs, and in the Federal Travel Regulation, 41 CFR Part 301-73, Travel Programs. Note: GSA is in the process of recodifying the FPMR in the Federal Management Regulation (FMR) at 41 CFR Chapter 102.

6. Authority to use GSA sources of supply and services. The authority to use GSA sources of supply and services is established by statute (see par. 7) or regulation.

7. Eligible activities. Organizations are eligible to use GSA sources of supply and services pursuant to the Property Act or other statutory authority. Please note that although an organization may be eligible to use GSA sources of supply, particular sources may not be accessible. In some cases, as resources or assets may not be available (especially in the case of the GSA Fleet), it may not be practical for GSA to make certain sources of supply available, or the contract(s) for the requested commodity or service may not permit participation by certain otherwise eligible organizations. Also, some organizations may be eligible to use only specific GSA sources of supply or services.

a. Executive agencies. Subsections 201(a) and 211(b) of the Property Act provide for executive agencies' use of GSA sources of supply and services. Executive agencies, as defined in subsection 3(a) of the Property Act, are:

(1) Executive departments. These are the cabinet departments defined in 5 U.S.C. 101 and are listed in App. A.

(2) Wholly owned Government corporations. These are defined in 31 U.S.C. 9101 and are listed in App. A.

(3) Independent establishments in the executive branch of the Government. These are generally defined by 5 U.S.C. 104. However, it is often necessary to consult specific statutes, legislative histories, and other references to determine whether a particular establishment is within the executive branch. To the extent that GSA has made such determinations, the organizations qualifying under this authority are listed in App. A.

b. Other Federal agencies, mixed-ownership Government corporations, the District of Columbia, and qualified nonprofit agencies

for the blind or other severely handicapped for use in making or
providing an approved commodity or service to the Government. Subsection 201(b) of the Property Act authorizes the Administrator to provide GSA sources of supply and services to these organizations upon request. Subsection 211(b) authorizes the Administrator to provide motor pool/GSA Fleet vehicles and related services to Federal agencies, mixed-ownership Government corporations, and the District of Columbia.

(1) Other Federal agencies. These are Federal agencies defined in subsection 3(b) of the Property Act that are not in the executive branch of the Government, i.e., any establishment in the legislative or judicial branch of the Government (except the Senate, the House of Representatives, and the Architect of the Capitol and any activities under his direction). To the extent that GSA has made such determinations, the organizations qualifying under this authority are listed in App. B.

(2) Mixed-ownership Government corporations. These are identified in 31 U.S.C. 9101. They are listed in App. B.

(3) District of Columbia. The Government of the District of Columbia is eligible to use GSA sources of supply and services. The Government of the District of Columbia and those parts thereof that have been determined eligible to use GSA sources of supply and services are listed in App. B.

c. The Senate, the House of Representatives, and activities under the direction of the Architect of the Capitol. These organizations are eligible to use GSA sources of supply and services under subsection 602(e) of the Property Act, upon request. To the extent that GSA has determined that various activities qualify under this authority, they are listed in App. B.

d. Other organizations authorized under the authority of the Property Act. GSA has further determined under the Property Act that certain other types of organizations are eligible to use its sources of supply and services.

(1) Cost-reimbursement contractors (and sub-contractors) as properly authorized. Under section 201 of the Federal Property and

Administrative Services Act of 1949, as amended, the Administrator determined that in order to promote greater economy and efficiency in Government procurement programs, contractors performing cost-reimbursement type contracts or other types of negotiated contracts, when the agency determines that a substantial dollar portion is of a cost-reimbursement nature, may be authorized to use GSA sources of supply. This authorization is reflected in Part 51 of the Federal Acquisition Regulation (FAR), which provides that agencies may authorize certain contractors (generally cost-reimbursement contractors) to use GSA sources of supply. In each case, the written authorization must conform to the requirements of FAR Part 51, Use of Government Sources by Contractors. Contractors are not eligible to obtain GSA city-pair contract airfares.

(2) Cost-reimbursement or fixed price contractors' use of GSA Fleet vehicles. Subpart 51.2 of the FAR states that, if it is in the Government's interest, a contracting officer may authorize a cost-reimbursement contractor to obtain, for official purposes only, GSA Fleet vehicles and related services. The FAR also states that Government contractors shall not be authorized to use GSA Fleet vehicles and related services for use in performance of any contract other than a cost-reimbursement contract, except as otherwise specifically approved by the Administrator. Accordingly, any request for use of GSA Fleet vehicles and related services by other than a cost-reimbursement contractor must be requested by the agency contracting officer and approved by GSA.

(3) Fixed-price contractors (and sub-contractors) purchasing security equipment. Under subsection 201(a) of the Property Act, the Administrator has determined that fixed-price contractors and lower-tier sub-contractors who are required to maintain custody of security classified records and information may purchase security equipment from GSA. Procedures for such acquisitions are set forth in FPMR 101-26.507.

(4) Non-Federal firefighting organizations cooperating with the Forest Service. Under section 201 of the Property Act, it has been determined that certain non-Federal firefighting organizations may purchase wildfire suppression equipment and supplies from the Federal Supply Service (FSS) (Article V, Agreement No. FSS 87-1, May 26, 1987).

(5) <u>Tribes and Tribal Organizations</u>. As provided in section 102(13) of Pub. L. 103-413 (the Indian Self-Determination Act Amendments of 1994), a tribal organization, when carrying out a contract, grant or cooperative agreement under the Indian Self-Determination and Education Assistance Act, is deemed an executive agency for purposes of subsection 201(a) of the Property Act. (25 U.S.C. § 450j(k)). Additionally, if the self-determination contract contains a provision authorizing interagency motor pool vehicles and related services, as provided in section 103 of the Indian Self-Determination Act Amendments of 1994, the tribe or tribal organization is eligible to use GSA Fleet vehicles and related services, if available. (25 U.S.C. § 4501) (Authorization to use GSA sources of supply under the authority cited in this paragraph does not include purchases for resale unless the contract, grant, cooperative agreement, or funding agreement authorizes such activity. Information on the authority for resale must be provided to GSA, and based on that information, GSA must concur.)

e. <u>Other statutes</u>. Other statutes authorize specific organizations to use GSA sources of supply and services. The organizations that have had eligibility reviews conducted and that have been determined eligible to use GSA sources of supply are listed in App. B or App. C, as appropriate. The major categories of such organizations include:

(1) <u>Certain institutions</u>. Pursuant to Pub. L. 95-355, the following activities are eligible to use GSA sources of supply and services and are listed in App. B:

(a) Howard University

(b) Gallaudet University

(c) National Technical Institute for the Deaf, and

(d) American Printing House for the Blind.

(2) <u>Insular governments</u>. As provided in section 302 of Pub. L. 102-247, (the Omnibus Insular Areas Act of 1992), the governments of American Samoa, Guam, the Northern Mariana Islands, and the Virgin Islands are eligible to use GSA sources of supply and services (48 U.S.C. § 1469e). These governments are listed in App. B.

(3) Entities authorized under the Foreign Assistance Act. Section 607 of the Foreign Assistance Act of 1961, as amended, 22 U.S.C. 2357, provides that the President may authorize friendly countries, international organizations, the American Red Cross, and voluntary nonprofit relief agencies to use GSA sources of supply and services when determined consistent with and in furtherance of the international development goals of the Foreign Assistance Act. Entities determined eligible under this authority are included in App. C. Purchases made by such entities through GSA sources of supply and services must be for civilian use only.

(4) Non-appropriated fund activities. FPMR 101-26.000 provides that military commissaries and non-appropriated fund activities may use GSA sources of supply and services for their own use, not for resale, unless otherwise authorized by the individual Federal agency and concurred in by GSA.

8. Ineligible activities. Except for the acquisition of excess personal property through sponsoring agencies, Federal grantees are ineligible to use GSA sources of supply and services. In addition, a cost-reimbursement contractor cannot transfer procurement authorization to a third party leasing company to use GSA sources of supply and services, unless the leasing company has an independent authorization to use GSA contracts.

9. Travel. Activities or organizations seeking to use GSA sources of supply and services for travel/transportation related services must obtain a separate determination for the requested service(s). This is necessary to determine whether or not the requesting entity is eligible under the language of the specific contract(s); e.g., travel management center services, travel charge card services, and air passenger transportation.

10. Excess, surplus, and forfeited property. The eligibility of activities and organizations to obtain supplies and services through GSA's personal property utilization and disposal programs is governed by FPMR Parts 101-42 through 101-46, 101-48, 101-49, and not by this order.

11. Determination of eligibility. Activities or organizations other than those covered in the appendixes to this order may be eligible to use GSA sources of supply and services. Activities or organizations requesting an

eligibility determination should submit their request to the Office of Governmentwide Policy, Attention: Office of Acquisition Policy (MV).

 DAVID J. BARRAM
Administrator

Executive Agencies

The following have been determined to be "executive agencies," or parts thereof, for the purpose of using GSA sources of supply and services. This list is not all-inclusive; other activities also may be eligible to use GSA sources, and GSA will rule on a case-by-case basis in response to requests received
(see par. 11). Listed here are major Federal activities and their subordinate entities about which inquiries have been received.

African Development Foundation
Agency for International Development
Agriculture, Department of
Air Force, Department of
American Battle Monuments Commission
Armed Forces Retirement Home
Army Corp of Engineers
Army, Department of
Bonneville Power Administration
Bureau of Land Management
Central Intelligence Agency
Christopher Columbus Fellowship Foundation
Commerce, Department of
Commission on Civil Rights
Commission on Fine Arts
Commodity Credit Corporation
Commodity Futures Trading Commission
Consumer Products Safety Commission
Corporation for National Community Service
Defense, Department of
Defense agencies and Joint Service Schools
Defense Nuclear Facilities Safety Board
Education, Department of
Energy, Department of
Environmental Protection Agency

Equal Employment Opportunity Commission
Executive Office of the President
Export-Import Bank of U.S.
Farm Credit Administration
Federal Communications Commission
Federal Election Commission
Federal Maritime Commission
Federal Trade Commission
Forest Service, U.S.
General Services Administration
Government National Mortgage Association
Harry S. Truman Scholarship Foundation
Health and Human Services, Department of
Homeland Security, Department of
Housing and Urban Development, Department of
Institute of Museum and Library Sciences
Interagency Council on the Homeless
Inter-American Foundation
Interior, Department of the
International Boundary and Water Commission, United States Section
Justice, Department of
Kennedy Center
Labor, Department of
Madison, James, Memorial Fellowship Foundation
Merit Systems Protection Board
Morris K. Udall Foundation
National Aeronautics and Space Administration
National Archives and Records Administration
National Credit Union Administration (not individual credit unions)
National Council on the Handicapped
National Endowment for the Arts
National Endowment for the Humanities
National Labor Relations Board
National Railroad Passenger Corp. (AMTRAK)
National Science Foundation
National Transportation Safety Board
Navy, Department of
Nuclear Regulatory Commission
Nuclear Waste Technical Review Board
Occupational Safety and Health Review Commission
Office of Federal Housing Enterprise Oversight

Office of Personnel Management
Office of Special Counsel
Panama Canal Commission
Peace Corps
Pension Benefit Guaranty Corporation
Postal Rate Commission
Presidio Trust, the
Railroad Retirement Board
St. Elizabeths Hospital
Securities and Exchange Commission
Selective Service System
Small Business Administration
Smithsonian Institution
Social Security Administration
State, Department of
Tennessee Valley Authority
Trade and Development Agency
Transportation, Department of
Treasury, Department of
U.S. Arms Control and Disarmament Agency
U.S. Information Agency
U.S. International Development Cooperation Agency
U.S. International Trade Commission
U.S. Postal Service
Veterans Affairs, Department of

Other Eligible Users

The following have been determined to be eligible to use GSA sources of
supply and services, in addition to the organizations listed in appendixes A
and C. An asterisk indicates that special limitations apply. This list is not
all-inclusive; other activities also may be eligible to use GSA sources.
GSA will rule upon eligibility on a case-by-case basis in response to
requests received (see par. 11).

Administrative Conference of the U.S.
Administrative Office of the U.S. Courts
Advisory Commission on Intergovernmental Relations
Advisory Committee on Federal Pay
American Printing House for the Blind
American Samoa, government of

Architect of the Capitol
Architectural and Transportation Barriers Compliance Board
Bank for Cooperatives
Certain non-appropriated fund activities (generally, not for resale)
Coast Guard Auxiliary (through the U.S. Coast Guard)
Committee for Purchase from the Blind and other Severely Handicapped
Contractors and subcontractors—cost reimbursement (as authorized by
the applicable agency's
   contracting official)
Contractors and subcontractors—fixed price (security equipment only
when so authorized by the
   applicable agency's contracting official)
Courts, Federal (not court reporters)
Delaware River Basin Commission
District of Columbia, Government of
Farm Credit Banks
Federal Deposit Insurance Corporation
Federal Home Loan Banks
Federal Intermediate Credit Bank
Federal Land Bank
Federal Reserve Board of Governors
Firefighters, Non-Federal (as authorized by the Forest Service, U.S.
Department of Agriculture)
Gallaudet University
Government Printing Office
Guam, government of
Harry S. Truman Scholarship Foundation
House of Representatives, U.S.
Howard University (including hospital)
Japan-United States Friendship Commission
Land Grant Institutions*
Legal Services Corporation (not its grantees)
Library of Congress
Marine Mammal Commission
Medicare Payment Advisory Commission
National Bank for Cooperatives (CoBank)
National Capital Planning Commission
National Gallery of Art
National Guard Activities (only through U.S. Property and Fiscal
Officers)
National Technical Institute for the Deaf

Navajo and Hopi Indian Relocation Commission
Neighborhood Reinvestment Corporation
Northern Mariana Islands, Commonwealth, government of
Senate, U.S.
Stennis, John C., Center for Public Service Training and Development
Susquehanna River Basin Commission
U.S. Institute of Peace
U.S. Representative, Office of Joint Economic Commission
Virgin Islands, government of (including Virgin Islands Port Authority)
Washington Metropolitan Area Transit Authority (METRO)

* as cost-reimbursement contractors.

International Organizations

The following have been determined to be eligible to use GSA sources of supply and services, in addition to the organizations listed in appendixes A and B. This list is not all-inclusive; other activities may also be eligible to use GSA sources. Also, as stated in par. 7e.(3), certain entities may be eligible to use only specific GSA sources and/or services. GSA will rule upon the eligibility of activities on a case-by-case basis in response to requests received (see par. 11).

African Development Fund
American Red Cross
Asian Development Bank
Caribbean Organization
Counterpart Foundation, Inc.
Customs Cooperation Council
European Space Research Organization
Food and Agriculture Organization of the United Nations
Great Lakes Fishery Commission
Inter-American Defense Board
Inter-American Development Bank
Inter-American Institute of Agriculture Sciences
Inter-American Investment Corporation
Inter-American Statistical Institute
Inter-American Tropical Tuna Commission
Intergovernmental Maritime Consultative Organization
Intergovernmental Committee for European Migration
International Atomic Energy Agency

International Bank of Reconstruction and Development (World Bank)
International Boundary Commission—United States and Canada
International Boundary and Water Commission—United States and Mexico
International Center for Settlement of Investment Disputes
International Civil Aviation Organization
International Coffee Organization
International Cotton Advisory Committee
International Development Association
International Fertilizer Development Center
International Finance Corporation
International Hydrographic Bureau
International Institute for Cotton
International Joint Commission—United States and Canada
International Labor Organization
International Maritime Satellite Organization
International Monetary Fund
International Pacific Halibut Commission
International Pacific Salmon Fisheries Commission—Canada
International Secretariat for Volunteer Services
International Telecommunications Satellite Organization
International Telecommunications Union
International Wheat Council
Lake Ontario Claims Tribunal
Multinational Force and Observers
Multinational Investment Guarantee Agency (MIGA)
North American Treaty Organization (NATO)
Organization of African Unity
Organization of American States
Organization for Economic Cooperation and Development
Pan American Health Organization
Radio Technical Commission for Aeronautics
South Pacific Commission
United International Bureau for the Protection of Intellectual Property
United Nations
United Nations Educational, Scientific, and Cultural Organization
Universal Postal Union
World Health Organization
World Intellectual Property Organization
World Meteorological Organization
World Tourism Organization

Appendix E

Sample GSA Schedule Teaming Agreement

This Arrangement to Team ("Teaming Arrangement"), effective
_____ is between _____ ("Team
Lead") with offices at _____ and
_____, ("Team Member") with
offices at

_____.

WHEREAS, Team Lead is providing support to the
_____ [agency, government-wide, contracting
office, etc.] under its General Service Administration Multiple Award
Schedule Number GS-35F-_____, Order Number ; and

WHEREAS, in connection with this support, Team Lead desires to
acquire, and Team Member desires to provide, certain labor and/or
product support via this Teaming Arrangement using Team Member's
MAS Number _____.

NOW THEREFORE, in consideration of the mutual covenants and
promises stated herein, the parties agree as follows:

1. Team Lead will assist Team Member in obtaining work in support

_____.

2. Team Member agrees to provide a discount of _____ percent off
their GSA Schedule [schedule number] prices as shown in Attachment
I. [Provide an attachment with the offered products/services and
agreed-to prices by item.]

3. Terms and conditions of any purchase order issued by Team Lead to
Team Member will be subject to the terms and conditions of Team

Member's GSA MAS incorporated herein and attached hereto (Attachment II).

4. Team Member and Team Lead shall separately and individually report to GSA their respective revenue under this Agreement. That is, Team Member shall report revenue for Labor/Products at the prices it charges Team Lead; Team Lead shall report any price uplift (the difference between the price invoiced by Team Member and the price Team Lead charges the Customer, if any). Team Lead and Team Member shall separately and individually be responsible for payment of their respective Industrial Funding Fees applicable to said revenue.

5. This is an IDIQ type agreement. Individual purchase orders will be issued by Team Lead that will specify the precise quantities and types of products/labor to be ordered for a specified location.

6. This Teaming Arrangement is effective through _____. [delivery order end date or the end date of the Team Member or Team Lead schedule. Whichever end date is earlier.]

Appendix F

Sample Blanket Purchase Agreement

BEST VALUE
BLANKET PURCHASE AGREEMENT
FEDERAL SUPPLY SCHEDULE

(Insert Customer Name)

In the spirit of the Federal Acquisition Streamlining Act (Agency) and (Contractor) enter into a cooperative agreement to further reduce the administrative costs of acquiring commercial items from the General Services Administration (GSA) Federal Supply Schedule Contract(s) _____.

Federal Supply Schedule contract BPAs eliminate contracting and open market costs such as: search for sources; the development of technical documents, solicitations and the evaluation of offers. Teaming Arrangements are permitted with Federal Supply Schedule Contractors in accordance with Federal Acquisition Regulation (FAR) 9.6.

This BPA will further decrease costs, reduce paperwork, and save time by eliminating the need for repetitive, individual purchases from the schedule contract. The end result is to create a purchasing mechanism for the Government that works better and costs less.

Signatures

_____   _____

AGENCY   DATE   CONTRACTOR   DATE

BPA NUMBER_____
(CUSTOMER NAME)
BLANKET PURCHASE AGREEMENT

Pursuant to GSA Federal Supply Schedule Contract
Number(s)_____, Blanket Purchase Agreements, the
Contractor agrees to the following terms of a Blanket Purchase
Agreement (BPA) EXCLUSIVELY WITH (Ordering Agency):

(1) The following contract items can be ordered under this BPA. All
orders placed against this BPA are subject to the terms and conditions
of the contract, except as noted below:

MODEL NUMBER/PART NUMBER	*SPECIAL BPA DISCOUNT/PRICE
_____	_____
_____	_____

(2) Delivery:

DESTINATION	*DELIVERY SCHEDULE/DATES
_____	_____
_____	_____

(3) The Government estimates, but does not guarantee, that the
volume of purchases through this agreement will be _____.

(4) This BPA does not obligate any funds.

(5) This BPA expires on _____ or at the end of the
contract period, whichever is earlier.

(6) The following office(s) is hereby authorized to place orders under
this BPA:

OFFICE	POINT OF CONTACT
_____	_____
_____	_____

(7) Orders will be placed against this BPA via Electronic Data Interchange (EDI), FAX, or paper.

(8) Unless otherwise agreed to, all deliveries under this BPA must be accompanied by delivery tickets or sales slips that must contain the following information as a minimum:

(a) Name of Contractor;
(b) Contract Number;
(c) BPA Number;
(d) Model Number or National Stock Number (NSN);
(e) Purchase Order Number;
(f) Date of Purchase;
(g) Quantity, Unit Price, and Extension of Each Item (unit prices and extensions need not be shown when incompatible with the use of automated systems; provided, that the invoice is itemized to show the information); and
(h) Date of Shipment.

(9) The requirements of a proper invoice are specified in the Federal Supply Schedule contract. Invoices will be submitted to the address specified within the purchase order transmission issued against this BPA.

(10) The terms and conditions included in this BPA apply to all purchases made pursuant to it. In the event of an inconsistency between the provisions of this BPA and the Contractor's invoice, the provisions of this BPA will take precedence.

Appendix G

Commercial Sales Practices Format for General Purpose Commercial Information Technology Equipment, Software and Services

COMMERCIAL SALES PRACTICES FORMAT (CSP-1)

Name of Offeror: _____

SIN(s): _____

Note: Please refer to clause 552.212-70, PREPARATION OF OFFER (MULTIPLE AWARD SCHEDULE), for additional information concerning your offer. Provide the following information for each SIN (or group of SINs or Sub SIN for which information is the same).

(1)   Provide the dollar value of sales to the general public at or based on an established catalog or market price during the previous 12-month period or the offerors last fiscal year: $_____. State beginning and ending of the 12 month period. Beginning_____Ending_____. In the event that a dollar value is not an appropriate measure of the sales, provide and describe your own measure of the sales of the item(s).

(2)   Show your total projected annual sales to the Government under this contract for the contract term, excluding options, for each SIN offered. If you currently hold a Federal Supply Schedule contract for the SIN the total projected annual sales should be based on your most recent 12 months of sales under that contract.

Special Item No. 132-3   Leasing of Product $_____

Special Item No. 132-4   Daily / Short Term Rental $_____

Special Item No. 132-8   Purchase of Equipment $_____

Special Item No. 132-12   Maintenance of Equipment,
                          Repair Service, and Repair
                          Parts/Spare Parts $_____

Special Item No. 132-32   Term Software Licenses $_____

Special Item No. 132-33   Perpetual Software Licenses $_____

Special Item No. 132-34   Maintenance of Software $_____

Special Item No. 132-50   Training $_____

Special Item No. 132-51   Information Technology
                          Professional Services $_____

Special Item No. 132-52   Electronic Commerce
                          Services $_____

Special Item No. 132-53   Wireless Services $_____

Special Item No. 132-60   Access Certificates for
                          Electronic Services
                          (ACES) Program $_____

Special Item No. 132-61   Public Key Infrastructure
                          (PKI) Shared Services
                          Provider (SSP) Program $_____

Special Item No. 132-62   HSPD-12 Product and
                          Service Components $_____

(3) Based on your written discounting policies (standard commercial sales practices in the event you do not have written discounting policies), are the discounts and any concessions which you offer the Government equal to or better than your best price (discount and concessions in any combination) offered to any customer acquiring the same items regardless of quantity or terms and conditions? YES_____ NO_____. (See definition of "concession" and "discount" in 552.212-70.)

(4)(a) Based on your written discounting policies (standard commercial sales practices in the event you do not have written discounting policies), provide information as requested for each SIN (or group of SINs for which the information is the same) in accordance with the instructions at Figure 515.2, which is provided in this solicitation for your convenience. The information should be provided in the chart below or in an equivalent format developed by the offeror. Rows should be added to accommodate as many customers as required.

COLUMN 1 CUSTOMER	COLUMN 2 DISCOUNT	COLUMN 3 QUANTITY/ VOLUME	COLUMN 4 FOB TERM	COLUMN 5 CONCESSIONS

(b)   Do any deviations from your written policies or standard commercial sales practices disclosed in the above chart ever result in better discounts (lower prices) or concessions than indicated? YES _____ NO_____. If YES, explain deviations in accordance with the instructions at Figure 515.4-2, which is provided in this solicitation for your convenience .

(5) If you are a dealer/reseller without significant sales to the general public, you should provide manufacturers' information required by paragraphs (1) through (4) above for each item/SIN offered, if the manufacturer's sales under any resulting contract are expected to exceed $500,000. You must also obtain written authorization from the manufacturer(s) for Government access, at any time before award or before agreeing to a modification, to the manufacturer's sales records for the purpose of verifying the information submitted by the manufacturer. The information is required in order to enable the Government to make a determination that the offered price is fair and reasonable. To expedite the review and processing of offers, you should advise the manufacturer(s) of this requirement. The contracting officer may require the information be submitted on electronic media with commercially available spreadsheet(s). The information may be provided by the manufacturer directly to the Government. If the

manufacturer's item(s) is being offered by multiple dealers/resellers, only one copy of the requested information should be submitted to the Government. In addition, you must submit the following information along with a listing of contact information regarding each of the manufacturers whose products and/or services are included in the offer (include the manufacturer's name, address, the manufacturer's contact point, telephone number, and FAX number) for each model offered by SIN:

(a)   Manufacturer's Name

(b)   Manufacturer's Part Number

(c)   Dealer's/Reseller's Part Number

(d)   Product Description

(e)   Manufacturer's List Price

(f)   Dealer's/Reseller's percentage discount from List Price or net prices

Figure 515.4-2-Instructions for Commercial Sales Practices Format

If you responded "YES" to question (3), on the COMMERCIAL SALES PRACTICES FORMAT, complete the chart in question (4)(a) for the customer(s) who receive your best discount. If you responded "NO" complete the chart in question (4)(a) showing your written policies or standard sales practices for all customers or customer categories to whom you sell at a price (discounts and concessions in combination) that is equal to or better than the price(s) offered to the Government under this solicitation or with which the Offeror has a current agreement to sell at a discount which equals or exceeds the discount(s) offered under this solicitation. Such agreement shall be in effect on the date the offer is submitted or contain an effective date during the proposed multiple award schedule contract period. If your offer is lower than your price to other customers or customer categories, you will be aligned with the customer or category of customer that receives your best price for purposes of the Price Reduction clause at 552.238-75. The Government expects you to provide information required by the format in accordance with these instructions that is, to the best of your knowledge and belief, current, accurate, and complete as of 14 calendar days prior to its submission. You must also disclose any changes in your price list(s), discounts and/or discounting policies which occur after the offer is submitted, but before the close of negotiations. If your discount practices vary by model or product line, the discount information should be by model or product line as appropriate. You may limit the number of models or product lines reported to those which exceed 75% of actual historical Government sales (commercial sales may be substituted if Government sales are unavailable) value of the special item number (SIN).

Column 1-Identify the applicable customer or category of customer. A "customer" is any entity, except the Federal Government, which acquires supplies or services from the Offeror. The term customer includes, but is not limited to original equipment manufacturers, value added resellers, state and local governments, distributors, educational institutions (an elementary, junior high, or degree granting school which maintains a regular faculty and established curriculum and an organized body of students), dealers, national accounts, and end users. In any instance where the Offeror is asked to disclose information for a customer, the Offeror may disclose information by category of customer if the offeror's discount policies or practices are the same for all customers in the category. (Use a separate line for each customer or category of customer.)

Column 2-Identify the discount. The term "discount" is as defined in solicitation clause 552.212-70, Preparation of Offer (Multiple Award Schedule). Indicate the best discount (based on your written discounting policies or standard commercial discounting practices if you do not have written discounting policies) at which you sell to the customer or category of customer identified in column 1, without regard to quantity; terms and conditions of the agreements under which the discounts are given; and whether the agreements are written or oral. Net prices or discounts off of other price lists should be expressed as percentage discounts from the price list which is the basis of your offer. If the discount disclosed is a combination of various discounts (prompt payment, quantity, etc.), the percentage should be broken out for each type of discount. If the price lists which are the basis of the discounts given to the customers identified in the chart are different than the price list submitted upon which your offer is based, identify the type or title and date of each price list. The contracting officer may require submission of these price lists. To expedite evaluation, offerors may provide these price lists at the time of submission.

Column 3-Identify the quantity or volume of sales. Insert the minimum quantity or sales volume which the identified customer or category of customer must either purchase/order, per order or within a specified period, to earn the discount. When purchases/orders must be placed within a specified period to earn a discount indicate the time period.

Column 4-Indicate the FOB delivery term for each identified customer. See FAR 47.3 for an explanation of FOB delivery terms.

Column 5-Indicate concessions regardless of quantity granted to the identified customer or category of customer. Concessions are defined in solicitation clause 552.212-70, Preparation of Offers (Multiple Award Schedule). If the space provided is inadequate, the disclosure should be made on a separate sheet by reference.

If you respond "YES" to question 4 (b) in the Commercial Sales Practices Format, provide an explanation of the circumstances under which you deviate from your written policies or standard commercial sales practices disclosed in the chart on the Commercial Sales Practices Format and explain how often they occur. Your explanation should include a discussion of situations that lead to deviations from standard practice, an explanation of how often they occur, and the controls you employ to assure the integrity of your pricing. Examples of typical deviations may include, but are not limited to, one time goodwill discounts to charity organizations or to compensate an otherwise disgruntled customer; a limited sale of obsolete or damaged goods; the sale of sample goods to a new customer; or the sales of prototype goods for testing purposes.

If deviations from your written policies or standard commercial sales practices disclosed in the chart on the Commercial Sales Practices Format are so significant and/or frequent that the Contracting Officer cannot establish whether the price(s) offered is fair and reasonable, then you may be asked to provide additional information. The Contracting Officer may ask for information to demonstrate that you have made substantial sales of the item(s) in the commercial market consistent with the information reflected on the chart on the Commercial Sales Practice Format, a description of the conditions surrounding those sales deviations, or other information that may be necessary in order for the Contracting Officer to determine whether your offered price(s) is fair and reasonable. In cases where additional information is requested, the Contracting Officer will target the request in order to limit the submission of data to that needed to establish the reasonableness of the offered price.